WITH THE GUNS

WITH THE GUNS

BY

F. O. O.

1916

TO
D. C.

CONTENTS

WITH THE GUNS

I

ARTILLERY

As these sketches of the changing phases of modern war are largely concerned with the work of the artillery, as, indeed, they are written from the standpoint of that branch of the Service, this would seem to be a favourable place to explain shortly the significance of the arm. My excuse, if any be needed, may be sought in the mind of the average man who, terrified as ever of the contemplation of anything technical, puzzled by the grandiloquence of the self-appointed " expert," regards the art of the artilleryman as written in a book sealed to him for ever by its own abstruseness.

Yet the general principles that guide the employment of the man with the gun, as distinguished from the man with the rifle, are very simple. In the first place, whereas the

latter is only concerned with the incapaci-
tating of *personnel*, the former has in addition
the task of the destruction of *matériel*. The
old and still popular idea of a battle, wherein
each arm engages exclusively the similar
arm of the enemy, has, since the middle of
the last century, entirely disappeared. In
a few words it may be said that the function
of the artillery of the attack is to prepare
the way for the infantry assault by the
demolition of the enemy's defences, so far
as that may be possible, and during this
actual assault to prevent the enemy's troops
from leaving their shelter and offering resistance. The artillery of the defence, on the
other hand, must endeavour to check the
fire of the hostile guns, either by overwhelm-
ing the batteries themselves by a fire so
intense that the detachments cannot work
the guns, or by the destruction of their
observation posts. During the assault, their
object must be to cover the space over which
the hostile infantry must advance with so
continuous a rain of shell that they are
unable to reach their objective.

In order to perform these various duties
with the greatest attainable efficiency artillery must possess two essentials. In the
first place, it must be able to project the

greatest possible weight of shell in a given time, and in the second it must be capable of rapid movement from one point to another so that it may be rapidly brought into use whenever the need for it is greatest. Now, obviously, the heavier the shell to be thrown, the greater must be the energy of the cartridge, and the greater the energy of the cartridge, the greater the strength (and consequently size and weight) of the gun necessary to withstand the pressures produced upon its discharge. On the other hand, if a gun is to be mobile, it must be as light as possible, both so that it can be moved at the required speed, and also that it can be taken over soft or difficult ground. Mobility and shell-power are therefore naturally antagonistic, the two cannot be combined in the same gun. The modern army, therefore, carries a range of guns, wherein maximum mobility controls one end of the scale and maximum shell-power the other. The former is represented by the mountain gun, firing a shell weighing some ten pounds and capable of being moved with great rapidity over practically any ground that a man can traverse laden, the latter by pieces of ordnance throwing a shell whose weight approximates to a ton, capable of very slow movement over good roads and requiring elaborately prepared positions from which to fire.

Suppose, however, that we were to take a six-inch gun, that is to say a gun firing a shell six inches in diameter and weighing a hundred pounds, with a range of say twenty thousand yards. This gun will require a cartridge consisting of about twenty pounds of propellant, to withstand the explosion of which the gun must be made of such massiveness that it will weigh some seven tons. Now instead of requiring so great a range, we determine to be satisfied with a range of six or seven thousand yards. We now find that a charge of only some two pounds of propellant will give us this range, and that the gun can now be built very much shorter and less massive, so that its weight is reduced to a ton and a half. We have retained the same weight of shell, but have sacrificed range to increased mobility, and the fruit of our labours is no longer a six-inch gun, but a six-inch howitzer. But in the process of conversion from a gun, the howitzer has acquired a new characteristic. Owing to its heavy charge of propellant, a gun projectile leaves the bore with great velocity, and consequently the gun requires relatively little elevation to hit a target at any given range. A howitzer, owing to its small charge, requires a far greater elevation. Now a projectile reaches its mark travelling at very much the same angle with the horizontal as when it started on its journey. At a range within the capacity of both, therefore, if fired say at a house, the shell from the gun will tend to hit the front wall, whereas the shell from the howitzer will tend to drop upon the roof. This tendency, combined with their difference in mobility, determines the choice of a gun or howitzer with which to attack a given target. It may be added that by still further reducing the range to be attained, say to a few hundred yards, a charge of only a few ounces need be employed, and a weapon produced, capable of being carried by a couple of men, yet still throwing a comparatively heavy shell. The German *Minenwerfers* and our own trench-mortars are the representatives of this class.

All these various types and sizes of ordnance (the word " gun " is a generic term that covers them all) employ two main types of projectile, shrapnel and high explosive. Shrapnel may be considered as a sort of shot gun fired from a rifled gun. It consists of a steel case filled with round bullets except for a chamber in the base containing a small quantity of powder. The head of the shell is fitted with a fuse which can be set to act at any given time after the gun is fired. This fuse ignites the powder in the base of the shell, which projects the bullets from the case in the form of a cone whose axis is the direction in which the shell is moving at the time. Shrapnel, therefore, depends for its effect upon the destructive power of the flying bullets. High-explosive projectiles consist of a very strong and heavy shell, entirely filled with a high-explosive compound, and fitted with a percussion fuse that acts when the shell strikes anything. The fuse ignites a primer which detonates the high-explosive charge, and the body of the shell splits up into pieces of various sizes which are hurled in all directions with considerable velocity. This type of shell has a double destructive power, that of the high explosive itself and of the flying fragments. The Germans employ a compromise in addition, known as " universal " shell, which may be described as a shrapnel with a high-explosive charge, which can be used with either a time or percussion fuse. They have also combined with the explosive charge of some of their projectiles a sub-

stance which on combustion produces an
irritant gas with the property of attacking
the eyes, and thereby making a position
untenable, and have also added phosphorus
to produce incendiary effects. It may be
accepted as a general rule that howitzers
employ only high explosive, guns both
shrapnel and high explosive.

We are now in a position to consider how
artillery can best engage the various types
of target that offer themselves. The gunner's
dream, a mass of infantry in the open, is
now but seldom seen, and when it is no
battery within range can restrain itself from
hurling anything it possesses at such a
heaven-sent objective. The most suitable
method of procedure is to overwhelm it with
a cloud of light shrapnel, burst well above
and in front of it, so as to produce a hail of
bullets beneath which nothing can live. In
the case of the attack of a trench, the method
usually employed is a preliminary bombardment by light and medium howitzers, with
the object of destroying it and its occupants,
or at all events rendering it untenable, by
dropping high explosive into it; as soon as
the infantry commence the assault, the
field guns cover the face of the trench with
shrapnel to prevent its defenders manning

the parapet with their rifles. It has been found that wire entanglements can be most easily and efficiently destroyed by light shrapnel burst just above or if possible amongst them, followed if necessary by a few light high-explosive shells to uproot the standards without forming deep craters that would impede the assaulting infantry.

A hostile battery in position under cover is usually engaged with high explosive from guns or howitzers. It is impossible to count upon a direct hit destroying any of the guns composing it, although such lucky shots have occurred. But the detachments may be forced to remain under cover and the battery communications disorganized. Either result will put the battery out of action so long as the fire continues. The real difficulty of such a target is to discover its exact position.

Fortified positions such as redoubts and buildings may be destroyed by the high-explosive fire of heavy guns and howitzers; observation posts by guns, as they are usually small, and, speaking generally, it is easier to hit a small mark with a gun than with a howitzer, owing to the former possessing greater accuracy. A somewhat peculiar feature of modern warfare is retaliation, of which the general principle is that if the enemy incommodes one by the use of his artillery, one or more batteries are ordered to fire a given number of rounds into some place where his troops are known to collect, such as a town or large village behind his lines. Guns firing high explosive are most suitable for this, as the point selected for retaliation is usually beyond the range of howitzers. It is often desired, more usually at night, to prevent the enemy from sending reinforcements to his front line. To effect this end, a " barrage " is established, usually by means of howitzers, which draw a curtain of high explosive between the massing-place of the reinforcements and their goal.

The first concern of any battery, once it is in position, is to be capable of maintaining fire as long as it is called upon to do so, and whenever necessary. To be able to do this presupposes immunity from hostile fire, and, it having been found in practice impossible to secure adequate protection from determined shelling, this involves concealment, not alone from direct view from the enemy's positions, but also from his aeroplanes and observation balloons. It is comparatively easy to find some natural or artificial feature behind which to place a battery, but it is

B

almost a life study so to disguise that battery that it will not be detected from above. Pits may have to be dug to hold the gun and its detachment, spanned by iron rails carrying a load of earth artistically planted with shrubs and flowers, the inside of a hay-stack may be torn out so that a heavy howitzer can just be manipulated in the space so formed, an innocent heap of beetroots may conceal the long graceful contour of a sixty-pounder. Yet, however careful the disguise, unless the detachments themselves hide under any cover available and remain absolutely still when a hostile aeroplane is overhead, or if by mischance the tell-tale flash of the gun betray it, suddenly and without warning the heart-gripping whirr of heavy shell will be heard, and before there is time for everybody to find the dug-outs, the battery will be an inferno of unendurable explosions and deadly flying splinters. Then, happy the battery commander whose casualties are but slight !

If the battery is so concealed from the enemy's positions that it cannot be seen from them, it follows that neither can they be seen from the battery. In order, therefore, to be able to bring fire to bear upon any given point, the officer controlling the battery must have recourse to one of three expedients. He must either go himself to some point from which he can see his target, and from which he can communicate with the battery, or he must plot the position of battery and target on a map, and work on that, or he must have an observer in an aeroplane who can see the target and can communicate with him. The first of these methods is known as direct observation, and may be described as one of the most important things that the war is teaching, and the most absorbing phase of the artilleryman's life. The principles underlying the second and third are self-evident, and the details of their application too lengthy for description.

Finally, let me try to convey an impression of the gunner's performances from various points of view. The infantryman is the gunner's keenest critic, and here let me say once and for all that the infantryman is at the same time the hero and the decisive factor of every war. Artillery but exists to smooth his path to victory, on him falls every brunt and every hardship, the gunner is a mere accessory to his accomplishments. No battle and no war can ever be won except by infantry, superiority in any other arm is useless if the enemy's infantry gain the upper hand by greater numbers or efficiency. He therefore has a right to weigh us in the balance, and it is the Allies' brightest star that their infantry, after endless weary months of suffering under vastly superior gun-fire, know at last that behind them are men and weapons that daily exhibit their newly-won preponderance.

It is the prerogative of all good soldiers to grumble when they are satisfied and contented, presumably as a reaction from the cheerful and unmurmuring endurance of hardship. The infantryman of to-day, although reposing every confidence in the artillery behind him, still believes the gunner to be a man of bad habits and occasional lapses. It is no use explaining to him that the round that fell so short as to burst in his trench instead of the enemy's was merely an evidence of senile decay on the part of the gun, and it would be mere waste of time to attempt to convey to the clay-plastered working-party who are busy shovelling up the parapet that it knocked down that accidents will happen even in the best regulated batteries. I have heard higher praise bestowed on our efforts than that of a group of senior officers, who whilst walking down

a communication trench at night, contrived
so firmly to entangle themselves in the
telephone wire to my observing station that
it took a whole platoon armed with wire-
cutters to unbind them—they irresistibly
reminded me of the Laocoon when I arrived
upon the scene. Further, it is easy to understand that men who wade along a muddy
ditch to the prospect of five long days and
nights in a morass are apt to speak slightingly
of others sleeping the sleep of the just in
warm dry dug-outs a mile or so back.

The gunner, on his part, admires the
infantry with an admiration no less deep
because it is hidden. Of course, he lacks
soul, thinks the gunner, he has no imagination to see that yesterday's bombardment
of the enemy's trench, although it *did* send a
few splinters whizzing into his own, must
have a subtle and profound bearing upon
the issue of the war entirely outweighing
any temporary inconvenience it may have
caused him. Besides, he is an incurable
marauder, nothing that can be made to burn
in a bucket fire is safe for an unguarded
moment. Lastly, he *will* clamour for ven-
geance upon an offending *Minenwerfer* just
as the light is getting too bad for observation
and one's servant appears with tea. But—

one can turn in and dream of home in the knowledge that he is between oneself and the enemy.

It is interesting to follow the variations of German military opinion on the subject of the Allied artillery. Bernhardi, writing a year or two before the war, gives it as his opinion that the Krupp gun is slightly superior to all other weapons, as, at that time, before the perfection of the French " *soixante-quinze*," it probably was. He advocates the abandonment of shrapnel for " universal " shell, and throws doubts upon the ability of a German commander to use efficiently all the batteries at his disposal. The outbreak of war found the Allies, as regards " field " artillery, that is to say mobile ordnance throwing a shell of from fifteen to twenty pounds, in the possession of superior weapons in slightly inferior numbers. As regards " heavy " artillery, grouping under that heading all natures of ordnance heavier than a field gun, to every twenty pieces brought into action by the enemy we possibly had one. It will probably be the verdict of history that the rapidity of the hostile advance up to the Marne, and the ability of the enemy to establish himself, practically unmolested, upon a strong defensive line, were due entirely to this fact. Documents captured lately, however, have revealed that the higher German artillery advisers consider that, weapon for weapon, our guns have a slight superiority, and in numbers available upon the Western front a distinct preponderance. They also impress upon battery commanders the need of study of our method of concealment and observation, as being in many ways preferable to their own.

Of the gunner himself a few words will suffice. He is of a traditional type, big, burly and equipped with a vocabulary that has been known to fuse the delicate windings of an over-sensitive telephone. His gun, for which his terms of endearment are expressed in profanity, is his only care, in his spare time he will sit in its emplacement as in his natural home. The "limber-gunner," an old soldier selected for each gun to keep it groomed and immaculate, is jealous of his charge as he has been for all time, since the day when Alfonso d'Este of Ferrara hurled the brazen statue of Pope Julius II into the melting-pot wherewith to cast more cannon. Hear him discoursing to a group of youngsters on the regimental motto. " Ubique," he says, " ubique, that means, my sons, that whenever there's a scrap on you an' me an' the bloomin' old pop-gun's got to up an' trek an' earn our blessed rum ration doin' ten days' work in one." And I think he speaks the truth.

II

'O.P.'

THE mystifying habit of speaking in abbreviations, the result of a constant use of rapid means of communication, is one that is developed to its maximum degree in the jargon of artillery. For instance, " L. X.C. El. 25° 30', 15' M L ORD BYF 40'' " is a very common type of order, and is the form in which that order would be transmitted. Consequently, whether in writing or in speech, the Observation Post is invariably referred to as the O.P. What more fitting than that these two letters should stand at the head of a sketch that proposes to deal with some of the aspects of these same observation posts?

The modern battery is so concealed that the view from it is often restricted to a few hundred yards in any direction. It therefore follows that the officer who wishes to direct its fire must discover some place from where he can see the target he proposes to engage, and from whence he can establish communication, in practice almost invariably by telephone, with his battery. He may be lucky enough to find some point near at hand, such as a church tower, from which he can obtain the necessary range of vision, and such points certainly have the advantage that they usually afford an extended view. But far more frequently, especially if his target is a hostile trench only a few yards from our own lines, some point right up forward must be selected, for preference just behind our own front line. This usually involves the selection of alternative positions, both because the view from each is usually restricted to a very small section of the hostile line, and also in the not-uncommon event of the observation officer being shelled out of his post, the battery is out of action until he has established himself somewhere else. The forward observation officer (F.O.O.) is the eye of the artillery, it is his business to observe not only the shooting of his own battery, but also to keep a watch over the whole of the enemy's territory visible from his post; to learn by constant inspection every detail, to perceive the smallest alteration or movement that may give a hint from which enemy plans or dispositions may be deduced. Hence it is clear that the selection of a good observation post is one that demands no small skill and experience. Nor is this selection altogether devoid of humour. A battery arrives, apparently from nowhere, its officers have a bundle of unfamiliar maps thrust into their hands, and are told to go and find as many O.P.s as they require to see a certain prescribed area. " So-and-so will go with you, if you like, he knows all about this part of the world." So-and-so is eventually, after a prolonged search, unearthed from the one comfortable chair in his mess, it being, as he bitterly explains, the only afternoon he has had off for a month. We start, preferably along a road pitted with shell-holes that look disconcertingly recent. Our guide informs us with melancholy pride that two telephonists of the 652nd Battery were killed there yesterday. " But it's usually pretty healthy——" A small and particularly vicious shell whizzes apparently just over our heads and bursts a hundred yards or so away. We change the conversation. We come to a place where the road ends, and where it seems as though some lover of beauty had cut a narrow winding course for a merry little streamlet that murmurs con-

tentedly between its banks. Some yards
away stands what was once a house, but the
doors have been wrenched off their hinges,
the windows are blocked up—no loss to
internal illumination, for a dozen huge gaps
in the wall amply supply the deficiency—
and the roof has collapsed, leaving only the
chimney-stacks standing. " That might do
for you," says our guide, " 750th Battery
used it for months." " How do we get
there ? "—for the country looks suspiciously
open and deserted beyond our present retreat
behind the hedge. " Oh, they don't often
snipe here, we can walk across one at a time,
or there's the communication trench," point-
ing to the streamlet. Heroes all, we elect
a soldier's death rather than wet feet, and
the first of our party starts to walk across
the open. Before he reaches the shelter of
the house, zip ! comes a bullet with the ugly
sound that marks the rifle fired in one's own
direction. He makes a wild dive for shelter,
from which he subsequently watches us as
we wade, cursing its maker, knee-deep along
the communication trench, and exhorts us
to be careful to change our socks when we
get home. After much argument, we decide
that the house will suit us, and we splash
homewards through our clay-coloured rivulet,

by no means comforted by the thought that
this is the only safe means of access to our
new-found property, unless we propose to
go there before daylight and stay till after
dark. Small things provoke humour where
amusements are few. I subsequently discovered that the depth of water in this
trench was about two inches less than the
length of my gumboots, and that, therefore,
by careful progression, I could navigate it
safely. Whilst doing this one day, a large
dog, presumably frightened by a shell
bursting near him—although animals of all
kinds get extraordinarily accustomed to such
things as a rule—plunged into the water
within a foot of me. The wave of his impact overflowed my boots—they have never
been really dry since—and the splash soaked
me to the skin. As I stood telling the world
at large what I thought of war and dogs and
trenches, a gentle voice, near at hand but
unseen, demanded of me, in the catchword
of the day, " Daddy, what did *you* do in the
great war ? " A sense of humour will make,
even of war, the finest game in the world.

Frequently the guide is young and enthusiastic, apt to let his confidence outstrip
his local knowledge. A representative of
this type volunteered to take one of us to a

place from whence he declared we could see
a particular point that puzzled us. The
two set out smiling, and promptly entangled
themselves in a maze of unfamiliar trenches.
The guide declared he knew every inch of
them, and for many hours as it seemed the
two wandered in and out, like trippers in
the maze at Hampton Court. At last they
reached the ruins of a farmhouse. " If you
climb up there you can see all right," said
the guide. The unwary pilgrim did so, and
found himself, outlined against the evening
sky, gazing at the German trenches not
thirty yards away. My friend is the soul
of discretion, he hurled himself rather than
jumped into the security of the trench,
followed by a *rafale* of machine-gun and
rifle fire. Nor was he mollified by the words
of a choleric and indignant infantry major,
who came up and wanted to know what the
devil he meant by acting like an infernal
clown and drawing fire on his trench—I
soften his epithets. There was a marked
coolness between the three for many days
to come.

More harrowing still is the whispered
legend of two adventurous spirits who, in
the early days of the war, when the armies
were not, as now, divided by an unbroken

line of trenches, set out to seek for some
commanding position from which to survey
the surrounding country. At dusk they
found a piece of rising ground, that seemed to
promise the fulfilment of all their hopes. Seeing a group of men at work upon it, they
strolled up to them and enquired whether it
were possible to observe the Germans from
there. " I know of but one place more
suitable, gentlemen, and that is Berlin," was
the reply, and in a very short time they were
on their way thither. They had chanced
upon the headquarters of a German division !

The observation post once found, the
next step is to make it tenable. It may be,
if Fate is kindly disposed, the upper storey
or garret of a house, from whence through
a hole in the roof or walls the necessary
view can be obtained. Happy the man who
finds such available ! The alternative is a
straw-stack, on the top of which one must
lie, covering oneself as much as possible with
straw ; a tree, amongst whose branches one
must perch like a disconsolate and clumsy bird
for whom there is no close time ; or, worse
than all, a spot in some particularly exposed
trench, over whose parapet one pops one's
head at the longest possible intervals for the
shortest possible time, wondering the while

whether the man opposite will pull his trigger
before one gets it down again. Generally
speaking, all these latter are to be avoided.
Any sort of ruin is preferable, and the more
of a ruin it is, the less likely is the enemy to
sit up and take notice of it. It is as well
to make it as bullet-proof as possible, by
judicious strengthening with timbers and
sandbags. Anything more ambitious is
waste of time; if a shell of any size hits it
directly, it is coming down and oneself inside
it, despite the most elaborate fortifications,
which in this case only serve to bury one
the deeper. All one can hope for is a little
box wherein to sit and observe, proof as far
as possible from rain and bullets, and a dug-
out for one's telephonists, in which one may
take shelter oneself if shelled—that is, if one
is lucky enough to get there in time. The
most important thing to remember is that
the exact appearance of every single object
within view is known to the observers on
the other side, and that consequently it is a
remarkably sure form of suicide to alter the
exterior view of anything that one proposes
to occupy. A careful man, however, can
establish quite a home-like resort almost
anywhere. I have known observation posts
within two or three hundred yards of the

German trenches whose occupants have
lived in profound peace and contentment
for weeks at a time.

A church tower, or even the remains of
one, is an ideal place. It is, certainly, sure
to be shelled periodically, but the first round
is not going to hit it, and a rapid (and, for
preference, carefully rehearsed) descent into
a cellar or dug-out at its foot usually averts
a *contretemps.* Of course, as happened once
in my experience, a lucky round may carry
away the stairs or ladders inside the tower
below the observing officer, who then spends
a *mauvis quart d'heure* whilst the enemy
leisurely shells him. It is surprising, though,
how many direct hits from even heavy
ordnance a tower will stand without falling.
If no church is available, the tallest house
or ruin that can be found must be adapted,
by making a tiny slit in the wall or roof,
invisible at a distance of a hundred yards or
so, and rigging up a platform inside on which
to sit whilst observing. A very ingenious
method that I once saw employed by a
French battery was to make a wooden box
the exact shape and size of the chimney
stack of a cottage, and painted brick red.
The box was hollow and had small peep-
holes cut in it. One night they skilfully

c

removed the real stack and substituted the imitation one, which served them admirably for many months. In another case all that was left of what had been a fair-sized house was a wall facing towards the enemy. A neighbouring ruined village was ransacked for a dovecot and a long ladder. A band of amateur carpenters fitted the dovecot to the inside of the wall, as high up as possible, cut a small hole through the wall, and arranged the ladder as a means of access to it. I can vouch from personal experience for the comfort and general excellence of the completed work.

Of the delights of a certain pear-tree, behind whose ample trunk was a most rickety ladder, up whose rotten rungs one climbed fearfully—the tree was about seventy yards behind our front trenches, and in full view from the German line—I will not speak. As autumn pursued its sorrowful course we watched the leaves of our tree fall off one by one, until to the prejudiced eyes of the man who had to climb into it there seemed hardly enough cover to hide a caterpillar. Finally, when an enthusiastic sportsman dumped a trench-mortar—the surest thing in the world to provoke a long-suffering enemy to fury—into a pit some twenty yards away, we shook our heads sadly and left it to its fate. It stands there still, waving its bare arms mockingly at us, but I, for one, shall not tempt its embraces until May has seen fit to dress it decently again.

The enemy, on his side, is no less ingenious and probably more painstaking. There was a certain water-tower that stood in a wood, with its top just visible above the surrounding trees. Imperceptibly, as the days went by, it seemed to grow out of the wood, until a month or so after we first noticed it, about ten feet of it were visible. The solution appears to have been that, to increase the field of view, all the trees in front of it, and there must have been two or three hundred of them, were very cautiously pruned every night, so as to show no apparent alteration from day to day, but gradually to allow the required observation.

It sometimes happens that it is necessary for the observing officer to remain night and day in the post, and under such circumstances continual interest is necessary if life is not to become very dull. Frequently the enemy are good enough to provide this interest, an unexpected shell now and again either just over or just short is a powerful antidote against ennui. More often our

own headquarters, with a laudable intention
of preventing one's interest from flagging,
send one encouraging messages—" Can you
see a hostile working party at such-and-such
a place ? If so, kindly keep under observation and report half-hourly," or " Infantry
report flashes of hostile battery in the direction of Hill 0, observe and locate if possible." One observes till one's eyes ache
as the light grows too bad to see, when a
second message comes, " Flashes reported
by infantry ascertained to be caused by
summer lightning." At night one crawls
into the dug-out and endeavours to slumber
with one ear glued to the telephone, and,
strangely enough, despite the presence of
two loud-sleeping telephonists, one usually
does.

Or perhaps it is only necessary for the
observing officer to be at his post during
the hours of daylight, which involves a
pleasant walk an hour before sunrise and
another an hour after sunset, both times at
which the approaches to the O.P. are being
shelled, or swept by a machine gun, or at
all events are receiving some sort of attention
from the enemy, who appear to take a
kindly interest in one's movements. Still,
this system secures one a night in bed, which

is a luxury by no means to be despised, and one is rewarded for one's early rising and walk by the prospect from the observation post during what is often the clearest part of the day, just before and after sunrise.   There, right in front, are the two lines of trenches, seemingly deserted, except where a faint curl of blue smoke denotes preparation for breakfast.   Over the whole space of country before one there is no sign of life or movement, unless perhaps at some point from a communication trench a spade-full of earth rises regularly.   In the middle distance over a cross-roads a succession of white puffs shows the suspicious nature of one of our field batteries, but further back still smoke rises from a tall chimney as though the world knew of no war.   The aeroplanes are up, of course, each cruising about in the centre of a constellation of greyish wisps of shrapnel, like flashes of cotton-wool against the greenish blue of the sky.   Rifles crack startlingly near at hand.   The drone of spent bullets rises and falls, the distant sound of guns blends with the bursting of the shrapnel far overhead and the hum of the aeroplanes. Surely all this noise is of another world, it cannot have any relation to the peaceful scene before our eyes ?   The treachery of the quicksand is the calm serenity of this Forbidden Land.

Observation posts have each their own legend, which clings to them through successive tenancies. We shared one once with a very youthful officer whose nervousness was only excelled by his ignorance. I fancy myself that he was only there to keep a claim on the place for his battery, but it so happened one fatal afternoon that he had to observe a series. The first round was fired, and the young man, suddenly discovering that observation of fire is one of the most difficult things in the world, and being utterly at sea as to where the shot had fallen, hesitated in his report. The rest of the tale is best told by the telephone. The battery commander is the first speaker. " Ask the observing officer to report where that round fell." "Mr. Jones reports that was a very good shot, sir." " Tell Mr. Jones I don't want criticism of my shooting, I want to know where the rounds fall. No. 2 is just firing." " Mr. Jones reports the last round fell about an inch from the target." " Then I can assume that as a hit ? " " Mr. Jones says he means an inch on the map, not an inch on the ground." Threatenings and slaughter *ad lib !*

Of course, it is an unpardonable crime to do anything in or near an O.P. which might draw the enemy's attention to it. A battery of my acquaintance had for some weeks been installed in a pretty little villa residence of which they were very proud, situated on the outskirts of a mining village. They had certainly spared no pains to make it comfortable or safe; indeed, the interior was a solid mass of sandbags through which a sort of tunnel ran to the little observation chamber, elaborately reached by a series of ladders and passages. One day the battery commander was conducting a deliberate and deeply calculated series, his mind too full of figures and angles to allow room for any idea of possible molestation by the enemy. Suddenly, directly behind the house, he heard a series of violent explosions. In rather less than the proverbial twinkling of an eye he was down below in the dug-out, nearly flayed by violent contact with ladders and other unyielding substances, but still alive and safe. Still the explosions continued, but no shell seemed to strike the house. At last one of his telephonists, more daring than the rest, ventured to peer out, and there, right in the sacred enclosure, was an armoured car in full and noisy action. The scene that followed baffles description. Two heads, one thrust through the hatchway of the car, one cautiously hidden behind a projecting sandbag, discussed the question of unmentionable idiots who wheeled their indescribable tin perambulators into other people's preserves, until the hardy navigators in the car and the stalwart gunners in the O.P. blushed to hear them. Finally, upon a reiterated threat from the major to turn his own battery on to the car if it did not move off, the nuisance was abated. But " Sans Souci," as we called the place, was never its old self again, its restful charm had departed. Some hostile battery had seen the flashes of the car's gun, and afterwards, at uncertain intervals, presumably when things were dull with it, would fire a few rounds in friendly greeting.

The gunner's appreciation of these things is usually keener even than one's own. One day when reconnoitring for an O.P. with a couple of telephonists, I came upon a house that had once been used for the purpose, but out of which its occupants had been driven by heavy shell-fire. The interior of the place presented an indescribable appearance. Its original owners had fled early in the war, leaving everything as it stood, and a succession of inquisitive searchers had been all through it to see if they could find anything of value. Dresses, broken bottles, letters, rags of all descriptions, a sewing machine, blended with the plaster from the walls and clay from the burst sandbags. Very little of the roof was left, and heavy rain had made of this mass a peculiarly evil-smelling mud, from which protruded here and there lumps of bread, bully-beef and cheese, whose increasing age was apparent. Some sort of cesspit had burst and flooded the cellar, which had been used as a dug-out, and in the centre of the savoury flood floated a mattress that looked as if it held the germs of all the plagues of Egypt. Outside, shrapnel were bursting freely, I fancy the enemy had seen us enter the place. I overheard one of my telephonists apostrophizing it : " You're a nice 'ouse, you are," he said. " Blowed if I don't advertise yer in the bloomin' papers, ' Charming bijou residence, quiet 'ealthy situation, perfect repair, hevery convenience, pleasant garden.' I *don't* think ! "

III

OBSERVATION

IT has been said in a previous chapter
that the fire of any given battery is, in the
majority of cases, directed by an officer in
an observation post from whence he can see
the target and the ground surrounding it.
The general principles of this observation
are as follows. The position of the battery
and target are ascertained upon a map, and
by means of it the range and direction of
the target from the battery are obtained.
A calculation based upon this information
is made, and a certain elevation and direction given to the guns. A round is then
fired, and the position of the point where it
falls relative to the target noted by the
observation officer, who gives a correction
based upon the error. This correction is
transmitted to the battery by methods de-
pending on the distance between it and the
observation post, but almost invariably by

telephone, and applied to the guns. Another
round is then fired, which is again observed
and a fresh correction made as before. This
process continues until the rounds are falling
at or very close to the target. It sounds
remarkably simple, but is in practice extremely difficult. To hit an unknown target
with the expenditure of the minimum possible number of rounds requires considerable
experience in observation, for the puff of a
bursting shell lasts only for the fraction of
a second, and is apt to look very small at a
distance of more than a few hundred yards.
Further, knowledge of the vagaries of each
individual gun is required, and also a keen
appreciation of the nature of the country
round about the target. Observation of
fire may be truly said to be an art, in that
it comes naturally to some people, whilst
others may spend a lifetime in its practice
without ever becoming proficient.

The second part of an observation officer's
duty, that of keeping a general watch on
the ground spread out in front of him, is
considerably easier, as it only requires a
keen eye and a good memory. After a little
practice, it is soon found that the apparent
changeless calm of a deserted land is in the
highest degree deceptive. Although they

are utterly invisible, that land is thickly populated with hidden troops, whose object it is perpetually to turn every feature of it, natural and artificial, to the best possible use for attack or defence. The ruins of a barn stand some little way back from the enemy's line, roofless and abandoned. The telescope shows it to have some part of its walls yet standing, and within them a ladder. Now ladders are precious things in a strip of country where everything is made to serve a useful purpose. Examine the place daily and perhaps at dawn a single figure may be seen scurrying up the ladder, or perhaps its position may have altered slightly. For weeks, perhaps, one has noticed a dilapidated house, so broken down that through the shell-holes that breach the front wall one can see the horizon beyond. Yet one morning one of these shell-holes shows dark, or perhaps a new one has appeared higher up, although no battery has been seen to fire at it. A flock of starlings pours suddenly from the stump of what was once a church tower, and for a long time the birds circle in clamorous flight about it, seemingly afraid to re-enter their accustomed haunt. Hints, all of these, indicating that some use is being made of these places, either as observation stations or snipers' posts.

Even the innocent-looking surface of a weed-grown field is not above suspicion. The naked eye is suddenly drawn to it by what seems at first almost inspiration, but one becomes conscious as one watches of an indeterminable movement taking place on its surface. Mark the place very carefully and bring the telescope to bear upon it. The sense of movement resolves itself into the periodic sprinkling of brown earth thrown up as by an industrious mole. These are spadefuls of earth, showing that a trench is being dug. Natural features themselves have a habit of changing their positions with the same disconcerting effect as that phenomenon had upon Macbeth. Of course, one is never lucky enough to catch them actually in motion, but a morning of surprises will often reveal the disappearance of a well-known hedge, or the sudden apparition of an orchard of full-grown trees in the middle of a ploughed field, or even a stately plantation of elms on what was formerly a *pavé* road. The hedge was removed to provide something with a field of fire, or to allow somebody to see a particular part of our line; the game is now to discover the whereabouts and nature of that something or somebody. The orchard and the elm trees were required as cover, probably for guns; the surest plan is to shell them and await developments. It may be possible to drive the detachments out into the open, when every weapon that can be brought to bear will sing its own particular song of triumph.

A certain redoubt was located by our aeroplanes, and its position indicated to us by the fact that it lay right in front of the seventh from the northern end of a row of trees such as occur at intervals along the side of most French *Routes Nationales*. For many days we used this mark, until it suddenly struck one of our observation officers that the trees looked somehow different to what they did when first he noticed them. Suspicion being thus aroused, further aeroplane reconnaissance was undertaken, when it was found that the third tree of the row now marked the position of the redoubt. The enemy, seeing that they had been " spotted " by the first aeroplane, had dug up the four trees at the northern end of the row and replanted them at the southern end, and must consequently have watched, with a delight not very difficult to imagine, our shells raising a little inferno of their own a couple of hundred yards away from them.

All this is a part of the great game of war that it is most difficult to learn in times of peace. " Pretending to look for something you know isn't there," as I have heard it described, is an occupation that palls upon the dullest mind. Well do I remember many years ago forming one of a class of young officers under instruction in the use of the " Observation of Fire Instrument," which consists of a telescope fearfully and wonderfully mounted on a gigantic tripod— it is now, in the language beloved of the textbooks, " becoming obsolescent," may it soon be relegated to the limbo of forgotten things ! Our instructor, a highly capable but choleric major (majors always were apt to be petulant, I thought, in those days), had spent the best part of a warm June morning explaining the use of the cumbrous toy, until the whole class were sick at heart. At last he sent one of our number some distance away with orders to observe and report upon some object in the distance out to sea, the while he discoursed to the remainder. The minutes slipped by, and no word came from the keeper of the lonely vigil. " Go and see what that dam! fool is up to, sergeant-major," said our instructor. Anon the sergeant-major returned, with a face as impassive as the metal of the instrument itself. "Well?" rapped out the major. "If you please, sir, Mr. Robinson is a-studying observation on the ladies' bathing-place!"

Observation, it may be repeated, is an art, but every art requires considerable training, if only in technique, before the artist can acquire perfect and instinctive expression. Where, as in the case of the art of the gunner, art leans for its support upon the strong arm of science, the probationary stage requires even more time and application on the part of the tyro. It has been said that it takes three years to teach an artillery officer the elements of his profession. It will doubtless be claimed as a triumph of foresight for our military administration that, although at the outbreak of war our heavy artillery *matériel* was, in equipment and numbers, such as would not inspire pride in a Central American Republic, we had a large reserve of highly-trained artillery officers and men languishing in the enforced sloth of our coast fortresses all over the world. Well it is for us that this was so, for this is a war of heavy artillery, and without these men to train, command and leaven the newly formed batteries that we were forced so hurriedly to raise, our artillery would never have attained its present admitted dominance. Splendid indeed is the new material; the artillery manage to secure officers of the higher and better educated classes, and men, thanks to rigidly-enforced physical standards, of the sturdier build; all ranks are full of the interest of their new profession, enthusiastic, keen to learn, absorbing in the sharp days of war knowledge that others required the leisurely weeks of peace to acquire. Still, may the country, in its just pride in the performances of these men, never forget the debt that it owes to that little band whose pay it loved to curtail and whose ambitions to discourage in the old forgotten years of peace !

But this is a digression, typical of the observation officer, whose thoughts stray into strange channels during the course of the long days of watching. How keenly he longs sometimes for " something to happen," especially during his first experiences of the work, before he realizes that something is always happening under his eyes, if he can only detect it. My own pet

D

longing was to see my first real live Hun
in his natural surroundings, a longing con-
ceived in much the same sort of inquiring
spirit that inspires the naturalist. I saw
him at last, he sprang from a trench in
which a shell had just fallen, ran literally
as if his life depended on it, which, in grim
earnest, it did, and dived like a rabbit into
a support trench a few yards away, followed
by cheers and bullets from our own lines.
My observation post was at that time not
more than a hundred yards behind our
front line, but, owing to the intricate nature
of the country, no signs of immediate war
could be seen except from the little slit in
the wall from which I observed. One day
I was stretching my legs in the road outside, when a staff officer, somewhat of a
rara avis in so advanced a spot, came by,
having evidently lost his way. Now a staff
officer was once defined to me by a very
distinguished regimental officer as " a being
whose natural common sense was buried
for ever beneath the vast mountain of his
own ignorance." This magnificent gentleman—he had probably been a distinguished
grocer, the pride of the local volunteers,
before the war—informed me that observation was impossible from where I then was,

and, indicating a ruin, the remains of whose roof could just be seen above the hedges, expressed his intention of surveying the country from its more favourable eminence. Bowing before his superior wisdom, I saluted and we parted, he to pursue the even tenor of his way, I to my seat behind the window to watch the fun, knowing that his objective was about half a mile behind the German lines. With an unholy delight, I saw him blunder into our trenches, exchange a hurried word with an officer who came forward to meet him, and then beat a precipitate retreat pursued by a most audible titter that ran swiftly along the line.

He took care to avoid on his return the Bath Club, as we called that O.P., from the number of flooded cellars it contained.

The study of nomenclature at the front is a very fascinating one, if only for the light that it throws upon the psychology of nostalgia. Every road, every communication trench is christened with some name around which hang the memories of the men who gave it, so that the native origins of these shrewd godfathers is never for a moment in doubt. Who but a native-born Londoner would have evolved a Harrow Road, off which, in an orgy of local geography, branch Edgware Road, Finchley Road, Maida Vale and a dozen other familiar names? Who but a young subaltern—his heart still unforgetful of the old *joie de vivre*, having established an O.P. at the end of a muddy ditch already known as Burlington Arcade, would have proudly labelled it " The Bristol," or who, but his envious friends near Shaftesbury Avenue, would have emulated him with " Maxime's " and " The Villa-villa "! Moray Avenue, Prince's Street, Deansgate, Dale Street, College Green, all tell their own story. And where association ends, description begins. Stink Farm, is, I believe, now marked as such on the official maps. Quality Street has already a place in history that may one day be shared by Mud Cottage, Canadian Orchard, la Maison des Mitrailleurs, Rue d'Enfer, and Le Tirebouchon. Sometimes the names of places have been anglicized almost out of recognition. Wingles and Hinges are pronounced as they appear to an English eye, Choques is Chokes, Gris Pot is Grease Pot, Lozinghem is Lozenges, to quote a very few examples. The same may be found on the German side. The Hohenzollern Redoubt is familiar by name to everybody. Near it is Breslauer Chausée

Loos contained Unter den Linden, Fried-
richstrasse, and, rather curiously, Ring-
strasse; Vendin le Vieil is Alt-Vendin, Lens,
Lenze. But this is yet another digression,
the wandering thoughts of the idle observer;
let us suppose him suddenly recalled to the
affairs of the moment by the insistent voice
of the telephone.

" Message for you, sir—from headquarters,"
says the telephonist, bearing a piece of pink
paper in his hand. I take it, and read,
" Fire twenty rounds at intersection of communication trenches at——" Here follow a
combination of figures and letters that de-
note the position on the map. " Very well,
call up the battery and give ' action.' Tell
them to report when ready." Out comes
the map, and the point mentioned in the
message found. A road runs east and west
close by it, yes, I know that road, have
often noticed it. A communication trench
runs along it for some way, then turns off
at right angles by a hedge, which it follows
for a couple of hundred yards till it meets its
fellow, which place of meeting I am ordered,
in the parlance of the front, to " strafe."
Can I see that hedge, I wonder? Prolonged
inspection through the glasses assures me
that I cannot. There is nothing for it but

to take a bearing.   One hundred and seventeen degrees from my position, five degrees left of the church tower.   Compass and sextant agree, giving me the line to the corner of a wood on the horizon, on which line my target must somewhere be situated. Out come the glasses again.   There certainly is a mound right in line with my mark in the centre of that meadow, but it might be anything.   Yes, the telescope shows it to be earth thrown up from some excavation or other, it must be the trench junction. It looks hopelessly foreshortened, nothing like the map, but then the map seems to look down on things with a calm judicial air, whilst I can only peer at them from their own level.   A very little practice in observation soon shows one that the human eye is utterly unreliable as a gauge of the length of anything that stretches away from it.   " Battery reports ready for action, sir," says the telephonist.   " Thank you.   No. 1 gun ranging, elevation nineteen degrees, etc., etc."   Back comes the warning, " No. 1 reports ready to fire, sir."   " Fire No. 1 ! " " No. 1 fired, sir ! " and then an eternity of breathless anxiety, during which all the fabled deadly sins of gunners long since condemned to everlasting execration rush upon

my memory. Suppose I have read the map
wrong, and that is not the place at all?
An instant's piercing scrutiny, which fails
to reassure me in the least. Even if that
is the place, it is not very far from our own
trenches. Did I give the right elevation?
Did I allow enough for wind? Were my
orders perfectly clear to the section commander? Did the layer lay correctly?
Shall I be " broke " if I slaughter a whole
platoon in our own trenches, or only shot?
. . . Eternity comes to an end at last after
a life of some ten seconds, and I hear the
whistle of the shell coming ever nearer—
safely over my head, anyhow, thank heaven !
Yes, she must have passed the trenches by
now ; where's she going to fall? The whistle
ends abruptly, but nowhere is there any
sign of smoke, nor does the sound of the
burst reach me. A blind, I suppose, the
shell must have fallen into something soft,
but I'd give ten years of my life to know
where. Well, there is nothing for it—" No. 1,
repeat, fire ! " " No. 1 fired, sir ! " The
whistle again, then right in line with the
target, and hiding it, a bright flash, a spout
of earth and a cloud of black smoke, followed
by a peculiar, sharp crash, and the hell of
doubt gives way to the heaven of satis-

faction. Such are the delights of observation.

And variously the excitement infects the blood of the observer. One will sit far back from his window, lest prying eyes should detect him through it, and give his orders slowly and methodically, weighing each carefully and making elaborate calculations the while, and occasionally exhorting the battery to care and deliberation. Another will thrust a telescope through a chink between two sandbags so that it shines like a heliograph in the morning sun and one wonders if some well-disposed angel has smitten the enemy with blindness for that every battery within range does not open fire on him. He, meanwhile, oblivious of such minor dangers, roars contradictory orders as through a megaphone, calling on the inhabitants of Tophet with strange formulæ because his orders are not obeyed before he gives them. I have seen a French Territorial battery in action for the first time in their lives, Mons. le capitaine subdued, almost tearful, but resolved to die in his O.P. as befits a soldier. His telephonists and assistants (he appeared to have dozens) equally anxious to see the fray, festoon themselves all over the building, hanging out of windows, clambering on to the roof, expressing their delight at the top of their voices. Eventually he restores some degree of order, and, rushing to the telephone, sweeps aside the operators, and gives the word himself. " Tirez, tirez, pour l'honneur de la belle France ! " The shot falls apparently in a totally different direction to where he anticipates. Again he rushes to the instrument, more perhaps in sorrow than in anger, and demands the presence of the section commander. " Mon lieutenant ! " he says, " ce n'est pas juste, c'est épouvantable ! Je me sens brisé ! Nom d'un nom, que vous êtes maladroit ! Dirigez la pièce encore vous même ! " He finishes his series at last, and as he turns to go, he salutes me gravely, saying, " Au revoir, monsieur, j'aimerais bien travailler ici à coté de vous, mais, hélas ! c'est fort impossible. Dans cette observatoire il y en a toujours de bruit ! " It must not for a moment be supposed that I speak disparagingly of the French gunners. They are, as a matter of fact, far better artillerists than ourselves, and we have much to learn from them. Possibly they lack something of our insular calm, as we certainly lack the vivid power of imagination and discernment that contributes very largely to their success. For this same calm the British gunner is hard to beat. On one occasion a heavy shell hit an O.P. fair and square, bringing it down in a heap of ruins. The observer, who by some miracle was not hurt, extricated himself from the pile of rubbish under which he found himself, and rushed down to the cellar, where he expected to find the mangled remains of his telephonist. There was the man, his hands full of fragments that had once been a telephone, standing with a puzzled expression on his face. " I 'ardly know what to do with this 'ere instrument, sir," was his greeting. " I don't see as 'ow I'm goin' to mend it without goin' back to the battery for some spare parts."

Observation by night is sometimes useful, as then the flashes of hostile batteries can be seen most distinctly. It is, however, a peculiarity of modern propellants that the actinic power of the flame produced on their combustion is such as to attract attention in broad daylight. I have had my eye caught by the flash of a ten-centimetre gun about four miles away at four o'clock on a sunny afternoon in September, and there is no doubt that this distance has frequently been exceeded. Still, night of course is the

best time, although then it is very much
easier to mistake the flash of a bursting shell
for that of a gun, and even if flashes are
observed, nothing can be noted except their
direction, their surroundings being invisible.
And a few hours at night in an O.P. have
their compensations. Over the trenches rise
continually the searching lights, throwing
everything into sudden contrast of light and
shade, making of the familiar scene whose
every stone and blade of grass one thought
to know by heart, a strange land of white
snow islands standing sheer out of yawning
black gulfs. Every now and then sharp
tongues of flame dart out from the parapet,
a sudden lurid flash in the air shows a
bursting shrapnel, or a brighter one on the
ground the more violent detonation of high
explosive. Perhaps a rocket signal of green
and red goes up, followed by a quicker
succession of flashes of all kinds as a patrol
between the trenches is discovered. Perhaps one may be lucky enough to see a
chance shell start a huge fire, such as burnt
once for three days and three nights in
Cité St. Pierre, producing a glow as of
twilight two good miles away. Whatever
may be seen, night has its fascination in
this strange world of sleepless activity as

much as in a land of quiet, but here its fascination is a stirring into life of eager pulses, a whispering in the ear of that ever-ready lust of battle that makes of war the finest sport that man ever devised. Somehow at night all deeds seem possible.

IV

THE FOUR DAYS

(September 21–24, 1915)

ALTHOUGH many descriptions and maps of the country round about Loos have been issued, it may not be out of place to attempt one more brief outline, from which the general trend of the operations from September 25, 1915, onward can be followed. Descriptions of a country that one does not know being invariably flat and unconvincing, it may suffice to lay down the main features in a very few words. From the La Bassée Canal southward to Souchez is a purely coal-mining district, one of the most important in France, an undulating country devoid of natural features, but abounding in artificial ones, such as chimney-stacks, mine-shafts and dump-heaps. The miners' villages, locally termed *corons*, group themselves about the pit-heads, and form two long lines of almost continuous brick and mortar, separated by a shallow valley, normally under cultivation, but now lying fallow and deserted, varying in width from a few hundred yards to a couple of miles or so. In the centre of this valley lies Loos, a village of some two thousand inhabitants, conspicuous for miles round from the huge double shaft, the famous Pylons, that rise nearly three hundred feet above the surface of the plain.

Of the two lines of villages, that surrounding the mines owned by the Compagnie des Mines de Béthune, and consisting of Cambrin, Vermelles, Philosophe, Mazingarbe, Les Brebis, Grenay, Maroc, and Aix Noulette, was, about the middle of September, held by the Allies. The eastern line, consisting of Auchy, Haisnes, Cité St. Elie, Hulluch, Benifontaine, Vendin, Cité St. Auguste, Lens and its countless suburbs, and Liévin, was, at the same period, held by the enemy. Along the course of the valley, but well up the western slope of it, so that the village of Loos lay a mile within them on the German side, ran the two opposing lines, with their maze of support and reserve trenches, their sinuous lines of communication trenches leading up the slopes of the valley to the villages in rear.

From our observation posts in Maroc the whole of the southern sector of these parallel works could be plainly seen, the line of each trench through the green overgrowth of weeds being conspicuously marked by the white chalk thrown up in excavating them. Behind these again, two long black arms stretched out towards us, with a sinister look as though inviting us to leave the comparative security of our trenches and rush to the attack of the body from which they grew, the city of Lens. In reality nothing but embankments formed by the continual deposition of refuse from the mines, these two arms, the northern known as the Double Crassier, the southern as the Puits XVI embankment, had been transformed by the enemy into exceedingly strong positions, mined, entrenched, fortified by every known means, the westernmost ramifications of the fortress into which Lens had been converted. Opposite the extremity of the Puits XVI embankment the Allied armies met, the right of the British line resting upon the Tenth French Army, the first of that great chain of armies that spreads, with one short gap, to the far-away Swiss mountains.

All through August and September the

roads behind the Allied front had been covered by infantry and artillery, and even towards the end by cavalry, all moving eastwards through the all-pervading chalk dust. Rumour, as ever, was busy with conjecture. This was merely a feint, maintained the pessimists, the real advance is to lie with the French in Champagne. Nonsense, replied the optimists, this is at last the long-looked-for general advance, the death-blow of trench warfare, the dawning of the millennium when the Battle of Position shall give way to the Battle of Movement, the beginning of the final struggle that will end only with the death-throes of the enemy on the Rhine! Whatever were one's individual opinions, the scent of battle, the glorious prospect of a " scrap," was in the air, and spirits rose accordingly.

Slowly, from the august sources wherein the strategy of armies has its birth, the true intentions of the Allies percolated. Looking back now, it seems that too much was allowed to be known from the first. Documents containing detailed programmes of the proposed operations were circulated in some cases as much as a fortnight before the selected day, and in the field it is impossible to prevent the contents of such documents becoming common knowledge within an incredibly short time, which is practically equivalent to sending the originals across to the enemy with one's compliments. It was subsequently established by the examination of prisoners that the German General Staff had full knowledge of our plans many days before the attack took place, and had, indeed, made dispositions to meet it. It is undoubtedly essential to circulate beforehand exact instructions as to the part that each unit is to perform in contemplated operations, but it is extremely doubtful if it is expedient to do so until the last possible moment. Apart from the danger of leakage to the enemy, it is always found, as indeed in this case, that the interval that elapses between the receipt of instructions and their execution is filled with a storm of amplifications, contradictions and amendments, poured out by intermediate commanders, until the unfortunate commander of a unit is faced, when called upon to act, by an accumulation of mutually incompatible orders. If a strong man, he throws them all indiscriminately into the fire, and, acting by the light of his own commonsense and initiative, stands a fair chance of succeeding; if a weak man,

E

he endeavours to act upon them all, and, with deadly certainty, fails.

The ultimate intention of the General Staff will not be revealed until long after the end of the war, if even then, nor need we concern ourselves with anything but the general instructions issued to the Fourth Corps, the southernmost portion of the First British Army, the army that held the line from the canal southward to the junction with the French. Briefly, these were to seize Loos, Hill 70, which is merely the eastern slope of the valley behind Loos, and to establish themselves on this slope in such a position as to command Lens from the north. It was understood that the French were to make a simultaneous attack from the direction of Souchez, occupy the Vimy ridge, and similarly threaten Lens from the south.

In order to attain these objects, a four days' bombardment of the enemy's position was to be undertaken, to be immediately followed by an assault upon the fifth day. Of the actual details of the targets to be engaged by each battery it is unnecessary to speak in a sketch of this nature. Our own battery, in common with the rest, was allotted targets to be engaged at different

periods of each of the four days, these days
being not specified, but described as days
V, W, X, and Y. Throughout a breathless
week we elaborated our plans, each day
bringing as a rule some modification of our
original instructions. We spent our daylight hours peering out of our observation
slits, and our evenings measuring ever new
angles and ranges on our maps, until each
one of us knew every stone in the country
that lay in front of us by some pet name,
and our maps developed strange diagrams
in every possible combination of coloured
chalks, for all the world like the diagram
of the London Tubes. Thus we possessed
our souls in a greater or less degree of im-
patience, till at last the message came :
" To-morrow is day V," and on the night
of September 20 I at least sought the genial
warmth of my valise feeling that the curtain
was about to rise upon the finest spectacle
that the world had ever seen.

That night was the lull before the storm.
All along our line the restless field guns woke
but fitfully, as a watch-dog to bark at the
moon, and then fell off to sleep again. Even
the incomparable French *soixante-quinzes* on
our right, whose voices are hushed neither
by day nor night, seemed restless, im-

patient, restrained, keeping long silences,
until in sheer desperation they burst into
uncontrollable passion, ceasing again as suddenly as they began, as though appalled
by their own act. Only the vivid lights
soared brilliantly as ever above the trenches,
failing, however, to evoke the usual saluta-
tion from their unsleeping wardens. So the
morning dawned, unheralded by the noisy
" morning hate " with which the opposing
armies invariably greeted one another, the
still air seeming to cower silently, awaiting
the shocks that were to come.

The spirit of expectancy had penetrated
into the battery itself. The gun detachments stood to their guns, polishing and
oiling for the twentieth time each smallest
detail. The men off duty stood about in
groups, talking in hushed voices, broken
suddenly now and then by a loud laugh
quickly checked, as men will when something is expected to happen. In the telephone dug-out sat the officers, silent save
for spasmodic efforts at general conversation,
starting nervously at each note of the buzzer.
At last a sudden stiffening of the telephonist
on duty, " Yes, I'm battery, yes—battery
action, sir ! " and the tension ceased. Instantly the battery leapt into life. " Right

section, lyddite, full charge, load! Switch angle four degrees right——" Strings of order pour from the section commanders, echoed by the " numbers one " in the gun-pits, dying away to silence again. Then the voice of the senior subaltern, " Report battery ready to fire ! " a breathless minute, seemingly interminable; at last a faint buzz from the telephone, the sharp cry " Fire No. 1 gun ! " and before the last sound of the order dies away the flash and roar of the howitzer proclaim that for us, at least, the Battle of Loos has begun.

So as the day passes on we fall into our usual routine. The battery is seemingly uninhabited but for the strident section commanders standing between their hidden guns, except when reliefs descend into the pits as into Avernus, out of which presently appear a knot of men dusty, grimy and incredibly thirsty. Sometimes an officer comes up to the section commander, stands reading his notebook over his shoulder for a few seconds, nods as he receives a terse word or so as to rate of fire, takes over the notebook, pencil and megaphone and carries on the ceaseless clamour. All the time, at regular intervals, the guns fire and the orders pass. Sometimes a keener note

is heard, " Left section, cease loading !
Fresh target——" and a new string of orders,
soon followed by a resumption of the periodic
roaring, as of a thunderstorm controlled by
an angel with a stop-watch. Or perhaps
" Fire No. 3 gun ! " and no instant report.
" What's the matter, No. 3 ? " " Missfire,
sir ! " " All right, look sharp ! " " All
ready, sir ! " " Fire No. 3, then ! " and the
rhythm commences again. After a time it
all has a strangely soothing effect on the
senses. First one loses the din of the surrounding batteries, then fails to notice the
report of one's own guns a few feet away,
giving orders mechanically notwithstanding.
Perhaps a stifled yawn and a glance at the
watch—is that infernal fellow never coming
to relieve me ? Then the warning voice
of the telephonist, " Fresh target coming
through, sir ! " and the wandering attention
leaps into watchfulness again.

Up at the observation post things are
very different. There the observing officer
sits, watching the black and yellow smoke
clouds of the bursting high explosive, or
the cotton-wool-like puffs of the shrapnel.
" No. 1 fired, sir ! " The words of the telephonists seem to come as from some other
world. Here she comes, far away behind,

the whistle of the shell shrieking louder as
she passes right overhead—splendid ! in the
very trench itself; see the black smoke spread
out and rise slowly from a long section of
trench, whilst the green vegetation grows
white with the falling chalk. No correction
can be made to that, " No. 1, repeat ! "
" No. 2 fired, sir ! " Here she comes, ah, a
little to the right—" No. 2, ten minutes more
left, fire ! " So it goes on, until this particular section of trench has practically disappeared, leaving only a white scar. Then
a change of target and a repetition of the
destruction. A fascinating business this on
so fine an autumn day, so fascinating that
all sense of time is lost, all conjecture as
to whether the enemy will take it into his
head to select our observation post as a
target is forgotten. The only thing in the
world is the measured fall of the shell and
the swift framing of the consequent order,
the only pleasure the deep satisfaction of
a well-placed round, the only despair the
haunting memory of a shot wasted that
might have been saved by a different
procedure.

During those four days of ceaseless bombardment, the enemy made very little reply
except at certain points; we subsequently

discovered why. He made no attempt to distribute his fire along our front line, nor did he make a systematic search for our observation posts, the vital organ of every battery and its most vulnerable one. Certain spots he selected, and with magnificent gunnery rendered them utterly untenable. Shell after shell fell with mathematical accuracy into Vermelles, Le Rutoire, Quality Street, but when once we had learnt these favoured spots, our casualties were very few, being avoided by the simple expedient of removing to places that appeared to be more suitable in the capacity of health-resorts, or, where that was impossible, taking to the cellars and remaining there.

Through four long days, from early in the morning until it became too dark to observe the fall of the rounds, the pitiless shelling continued, nor was the enemy allowed any respite at night. In the batteries we were then busy replenishing ammunition and overhauling every detail of the equipment, but still one gun per battery at least fired steadily throughout the hours of darkness, not now on the enemy's positions, but on his billets and on certain places through which his reinforcements must pass on their way to the firing line. A few rounds per hour only, sufficient to keep men crouching huddled in cellars wherein was no possibility of sleep, or to shake the *morale* of working parties faced with the necessity of running the gauntlet of that steady rain. The moral effect upon troops already shaken by bombardment is enormous, as we ourselves have had bitter cause to know in the earlier months of the war. The effect of these days and nights upon the enemy is vividly shown in the diary of a private in the Second Reserve Infantry Regiment (Prussian) which fell into our hands later. A few extracts will suffice. On the 21st he writes : " Towards mid-day the trenches had already fallen in in many places. Dug-outs were completely overwhelmed . . . most of them fled, leaving rifles and ammunition behind . . . the air was becoming heated from so many explosions." On the 22nd : " Shells and shrapnel (*granatschuss*) are bursting all round . . . in places where the trench had disappeared I crawled on my hands and knees amid a hail of bullets." On the 23rd : " Our look-out post was completely destroyed, and my comrades killed in it . . . even the strongest man may lose his brain and nerves in a time like this." On the

24th : " The fourth day of this terrible bombardment. . . . I am sorry to say that there is no reply from our artillery."

Other prisoners, on being interrogated, testified to the awful effects of our fire. Upon one in particular, an artillery officer, was found an order that revealed the secret of the ineffectiveness of the enemy's reply. After briefly setting out the measures to be taken in case of a British offensive, it goes on as follows : " Owing to the fact that the preponderance of hostile artillery in this sector is probably more than two to one, and owing to the vital necessity of economy in ammunition, battery commanders will confine their fire to targets whose importance is known to them, and upon which they can count on producing a good effect. They will under no circumstances allow themselves to be drawn into anything approaching to an artillery duel." It was also stated by many captured officers that during the night September 23–24 a deserter from our line had conveyed to the German Staff the time and date of the coming assault, and that to this fact they owed much of the effectiveness of the measures taken to resist it. Yet another captured document was of somewhat disconcerting interest to us gunners, namely, a map upon which was very accurately shown the position of every allied battery, with only two exceptions, in the whole of our sector. It seems fairly certain that this was due to the most efficient espionage, and not to aerial observation.

The material effect of such a bombardment is harder to judge, for it must be remembered that, despite the high science of modern gunnery, the percentage of direct hits upon a given objective is still comparatively small. When, however, a heavy shell detonates under favourable conditions, its destructive power is enormous. For instance, on the third day I saw a direct hit by one of our largest howitzers upon the boiler-house of Puits XVI. The shell penetrated the roof and burst inside the building, sending up an enormous cloud of black smoke tinged with the pink of pulverized brick, that hung for several minutes. When it cleared, nothing but a gaunt and twisted framework of steel girders remained, a heap of rubbish alone showing where the walls had stood. A smaller howitzer was ordered to fell a brick wall, some thirty feet high and many courses thick. The shell burst in regular sequence at its foot, at roughly ten yards interval, each round

bringing down an equivalent section of the
wall, until nothing remained but a long
pile of smoking rubble. And, more im-
pressive, perhaps, than all is the sight of a
medium lyddite shell bursting in a narrow
trench. Out of the centre of a vivid flash
fly heavy timbers, sandbags, revetments, all
that once formed the trench, sometimes the
mangled fragments of its occupants, whilst
to right and left rolls the choking smoke,
driving its way into the deepest dug-outs,
overcoming men many yards away from
the point of impact, spreading death in
every form. Is it to be wondered at that
when our infantry reached these trenches
they found a few survivors, living indeed
still, but struggling and raving as the
inmates of some ghastly Bedlam?

V

THE DAY OF ASSAULT

(September 25, 1915)

DURING the night of September 24–25, infantry patrols left the trenches to explore the condition of the enemy's wire entanglements, upon the destruction of which our field batteries had been engaged during the previous day. Artillery fire was therefore reduced as much as could be done with safety, and was chiefly directed upon reserves and billets, in order to make the chance of rounds falling short injuring the patrols as small as possible. During the evening the batteries opposed to us had shown far greater liveliness than they had hitherto. Possibly the enemy had got information as to where the decisive attack was to be made, as it seems to be the fact that owing to the four days' bombardment having taken place along the whole of the British front, they had hitherto hesitated

to reinforce any particular sector, but had
kept their reserves in a state of immediate
readiness at their various railway centres.
If this was the case, it is very probable that
during the 23rd and 24th fresh batteries
were placed in position between Vendin-le-
Vieil and Lens, and that these came into
action on the afternoon and evening of the
24th. This supposition is borne out by
the fact of the enemy's ability to bring a
terrific fire to bear on Loos as soon as we
entered it.

Until the light failed, we had been busily
engaged dropping shell along the Double
Crassier, upon whose grim black crest the
enemy were suspected of having mounted
a number of machine guns. I had been
in the observation post nearly the whole
day—it is, by the way, worthy of remark
as showing the immunity from retaliation
that we had enjoyed in our sector, that we
used to walk to and from our O.P. at all
hours of the day through country literally
covered with batteries, none of whom up
till now had suffered any casualties—but at
about seven o'clock duty recalled me to the
battery. So absorbed had I been in the
difficult business of observing in the failing
light, that although I was conscious that

shells were bursting all round, I had no idea that anything out of the ordinary was taking place until one of our telephonists, who had been out repairing the line, returned somewhat shaken, having been blown off his feet and thrown some distance by a high-explosive detonating close to him. His only complaint, I may say, was that he had lost a pair of wire-cutters in the adventure !

However, as soon as I started my walk homewards along the " Harrow Road," I found things still fairly lively. Several houses had been destroyed since the morning, and some very fine examples of shell-holes in the middle of the road added to the joys of the transport drivers, whose wagons of all descriptions were now beginning to pour along it. At one point a medium shell burst about twenty yards away from me— I had heard it coming and found friendly refuge in the ditch—and before the smoke had fairly cleared an armoured car and a motor cyclist orderly drove simultaneously into it from opposite directions. Nobody was hurt, but the road was most effectively obstructed, and the effect produced was exactly like that of a block in Piccadilly, including the language. I reached the battery safely, to find that the shelling had not reached so far back, but that another form of excitement had supervened. We had received orders to be ready to move at the shortest possible notice, in case a general advance upon the morrow should render a change in our position necessary. Of course, we had been prepared for this for days, but even so this official pronouncement of our hopes sent a thrill through every one of us. This was, then, the decisive struggle, the Waterloo of the campaign at last !

Moving a battery of heavy guns is, however, no small matter, and one that involves a vast amount of labour, not to be lightly undertaken. A story is told of a certain major, distinguished alike for his capability and his piety, who, knowing from bitter experience the difficulties that attended a change of position of his battery, added on this night to his usual formula of prayer these heart-felt words, " O Lord, grant us victory in the coming struggle—*but not in my sector !* "

I think that despite the fact that the guns were silent for the first time since the beginning of the bombardment, very few of us slept much that night. Our schemes were perfect, certainly, every detail of our actions of the morrow had been long worked out, each phase starting a definite time after an empiric zero, which we now learnt was fixed for 5.50 a.m. But—would the enemy consent to fall in with those schemes? Suppose they anticipated our offensive by an attack of their own? The wire in front of their trenches was already destroyed, even now our infantry were busy cutting wide passages through our own. How strong were they in reality? Was their passive endurance of our fire only a blind to lull us into security? These and a thousand other conjectures troubled our minds all night, and it was with a deep feeling of relief that we stood in the battery, no untoward incident having marred our plans, at 5.30 a.m. on the 25th—the eagerly awaited Day Z!

Then were the scenes at the opening of the bombardment repeated. Along our line all was again quiet, only from our right came the distant echoes of the fighting round Souchez and the Labyrinth, a deep roar that had now been continuous for over a week. Again we sit in the telephone dug-out, tense and expectant. "Official time coming, sir!" Watches are taken out in readiness.

F

" Five thirty-five—now ! " Quarter of an
hour to go ! One by one we creep out to
see for the last time that all is ready. One
minute more—" Hook your lanyards ! "
slowly the hand ticks round—time zero—
" Fire ! " This was no deliberate bombardment, every gun must in the short interval
allowed it work to its utmost capacity, every
man sweating in the dust-laden pits must
toil as he never toiled before to feed it; into
the luckless trenches in front of us must
pour such a blasting hurricane of fire that
the resistance prepared for our attack shall
wither away in its deadly breath. But
soon our own troops will be pouring out of
their trenches, charging over the dividing
ground to hurl themselves upon the trenches
into which our wrath is now being poured,
and then our fire must be lifted lest we do
more harm than good. All is arranged for
in the time-table. At forty minutes past
zero, or 6.30 a.m., every battery lifts its
fire from the front line to the second line,
and still the furious fire continues. But
now we know that the blow is being struck
—what would we all not give to be in action
in the open as in old days so that we could
see the assault, watch the joining of the
battle ? Unprofitable thoughts ! let us

rather devote every fibre of our beings to the only task by which we can help, the task of pouring an ever-increasing weight of shell upon the defenders. That morning dawned grey and dull. From the observing post it was hardly possible to see further than the front line trenches at half-past five, and until the moment of the assault visibility did not greatly increase. However, this was to be the battlefield, we knew, at all events in the first stages of the struggle. The expectancy of viewing the greatest battle in history was to our little party in the O.P. strangely *banal;* I, for one, could not grasp the reality of it; I felt as though I were in a box waiting for the actors to come upon a stage before which the curtain had risen prematurely. There was no sign of battle, no movement that the eye could detect over the whole of the wide prospect before us. And then suddenly came time zero, bringing with it a scene that could never be forgotten. From the whole length of our front trench, as far as the eye could reach, rose, vertically at first, a grey cloud of smoke and gas, that, impelled by a gentle wind, spread slowly towards the enemy's trenches, very soon enveloping the whole of our range of vision in its opaque veil. This was our view of the assault, this dismal vapour the aura that was to surround a thousand sacrifices, the cloak that was to hide a thousand gallant deeds, the winding-sheet that was to enwrap so many a hero. Modern war holds no dramatic spectacles to enchant the brush of a Meisonnier, no drama is wrought upon a lime-lit stage to arrest the pulses of the watching nations. Yet none the less is its fascination omnipotent; its magnetic attraction, that draws into its vortex every man that owns a soul to plague him, is none the less irresistible; its influence still has the power to weld a chain of heroes out of a dirty, blasphemous, footsore crowd of sinners. War tends to the uplifting of the race, not to its debasement, let him who has faced it deny it if he can !

At 6.30 a.m. the infantry left their trenches and, so far as we were concerned, vanished into the smoke. All we could see were the columns scaling the ladders and starting to double across the open. Some seemed to trip as they ran, and fell in various attitudes from which they did not trouble to rise. At first we thought that our wire had not been thoroughly cut, and that these men had fallen over some unseen strands. But the red pools that slowly surrounded each soon undeceived us, the while that the roar of rifle-fire from the enemy's side grew ever more menacing. We could not see what success attended those who went on, but we heard subsequently that practically no resistance was encountered on the enemy's first and second line, but that the third line was very strongly held and considerably delayed, in some sectors permanently arrested, our advance.

The battery and the O.P. were equally desirable as far as vision went, the battery being blind by nature and the O.P. by science. It has, incidentally, yet to be proved that the hindrance to the enemy caused by the use of smoke is not more than counterbalanced by the paralysing of the initiative of one's own artillery, who are entirely dependent, when this method of warfare is employed, upon time-tables and such messages as the advancing infantry may be able to send back. However, that is not a question meet for discussion except in works devoted to the abstruse study of strategy and tactics. Let us return to the passage of events in the battery.

Here hopes and fears fought for the mastery throughout the morning, in accordance with the portents of the day. An order to

lift fire on to a more distant point seemed
to mean that our attack was developing
against it, and the men in the pits paused to
cheer in the midst of their unceasing labour.
Then suddenly fire would be swept back on
to a point that we had determined in our
own minds to have been captured long ago,
and our spirits fell, the detachments setting
their teeth and straining at the heated guns
to force by sheer weight of metal the taking
of the disputed point. Or, saddest sight of
all, down the road flowed an ever-widening
stream of casualties, ambulances laden with
stretchers upon which twisted forms lay
very still, others with the less severely
wounded, and a motley crowd on foot with
minor injuries, supporting one another as
one imagines the scriptural halt, maimed
and blind to have done. I think that none
of us realized till we saw the magnitude of
this stream, how fierce a fight was raging
in front of us. If this sight hardened our
determination, the next procession went far
to cheer us. A few hundred prisoners were
marched past us on the way to the rear,
fine upstanding men enough, looking perfectly fit and in the prime of life, disposing
effectually, in my mind at least, of the fable
born of our national love for self-deceit that

the enemy were hard put to it to find men
fit for service.

The German batteries were now devoting
their attention to our advancing infantry,
endeavouring at the same time to create a
barrage behind them on our main arteries
of communication. The Harrow Road
suffered to a certain extent, but the greatest
slaughter took place on the Lens-Béthune
and Vermelles-Hulluch roads. On the former
the whole of a divisional train was overwhelmed by shrapnel, blocking the road for
a quarter of a mile with shattered wagons
and dead horses (a picture of which debris
subsequently went the round of the illus-
trated Press under the heading " Captured
German Battery at Loos "). Two of our
field batteries that endeavoured to come into
action in the open between Quality Street
and La Chapelle de Notre Dame de Consolation suffered very heavily and were silenced.
Of the losses of the infantry, nobody who
did not see the procession of casualties and,
worse still, the burial parties of the next
few days, can form an adequate picture.
" British Offensive in the West," we read,
" Gain of five miles of trench." Each foot
of that five miles cost us a life and a sum of
human agony such as this world has never

known. Watch that communication trench
marked " Stretchers to rear only." Here
they come, two stretcher-bearers, one limp-
ing painfully, the sleeve of the other growing ever darker with a purple stain that
spreads slowly over it. Between them
they carry a poor wretch with both legs
broken, whose low moan of agony rises to
a sharp wail at each jolting step. Supporting themselves on the shoulders of the
stretcher-bearers are two more, one with his
breath gurgling through a throat choked
with blood, one with a shattered shoulder
and side. Through the treacherous clay
that covers the bottom of the trench they
make their way of agony, reeling from side
to side as their feet fail to find a foothold,
cursing their Maker for the horror of their
torture. See, the first stretcher-bearer slips
—his wounded foot will bear him no longer
—and down falls the whole party in one
screaming, writhing mass. Two miles more :
is there no end to human suffering? is
heaven so pitiless? There is the answer, a
sharp whistle, a low report, a puff of smoke
just over the trench, and all is quiet, save
for one form that crawls very slowly on
hands and knees through the yellow clay
that grows dark crimson in his track.

In these terms must we reckon the price of victory.

This is not the place, nor is it within my ability, to give an historical study of the varying phases of the battle. Suffice it to say that by noon the 15th Division had swept through the northern end of Loos, and were engaged upon that part of the eastern slope of the valley known as Hill 70. There had been considerable street-fighting in the village, but the enemy had evidently realized that this was not the place to make a determined stand. Their strategy appears to have been to concentrate their forces on the edge of the valley, leaving within it only detachments of such strengths that the loss occasioned by their sacrifice would be altogether outweighed by the gain in time that they secured to the main defence. And nobly these detachments performed the task allotted to them. One battery took up a position along the Loos-Benifontaine road, and remained in action under a fire whose intensity it is impossible to describe until our troops were almost upon it, when its fire ceased, not from lack of courage to continue, but because no single man was left alive to serve the guns. Let us give the enemy his due, we are not fighting a nation of cowards and assassins, as we are so fond of trying to believe, but of brave and determined men, whom to defeat will call from us our utmost energies.

As soon as we had taken Loos, the enemy opened a steady artillery fire upon the village, in order to prevent its use by us as a *point d'appui* for further attack, and to hinder observation from the various landmarks it contained. There is so little natural cover that this must have been a serious disadvantage to us, as by this time the communication trenches leading from the German front line trenches that we now held up the slopes of the valley were choked with dead, and reinforcements had to run the gauntlet of a well-directed fire in order to reach our line of attack. This may have something to do with that fatal delay that left the attacking divisions unsupported and checked an advance that might well have resulted in the capture of Lens, which would probably in turn have sealed the fate of Lille. We have learnt from prisoners that the enemy anticipated the worst in the early hours of the morning, and that the feebleness of the final blow amazed them. Had fresh divisions poured down the Lens road through Cité St. Auguste and Cité St. Laurent, rolling the enemy back upon the French who were advancing towards Vimy, who knows what might not have happened? Conjecture is useless, regret of a lost opportunity must take its place.

The facts so far as known—and no two accounts, even of those who took part in the struggle, quite agree—are as follows: The 47th Division, London Territorials all of them, the heroes of the day, but of whose performances, because less showy, little has been heard, had by 9.30 a.m. surmounted a series of obstacles, the storming of any one of which would have earned them lasting fame. Like a tide they poured over the western end of the dreaded Double Crassier, utterly regardless of withering machine-gun fire, and swept to the attack of the walled cemetery that stands to the south-west of Loos. From here, after a titanic struggle, they dislodged the strong party of its defenders, and, gaining fresh impetus from the check, irresistibly fought their way through the outskirts of the village, in which every point of vantage was held against them, right up to its heart, the mine buildings that cluster at the foot of the Pylons. This fortress they stormed and won, and the rush of their assault carried them on its crest over the Loos Crassier—another high embankment of refuse and slag—over the exposed surface of the plain, into the copse that stretches westward from Loos Chalk Pit. Here at last for a while they rested, and here for the present we may leave them. May the great city be for ever proud of the achievements of her sons this day, the thousand forgotten deeds of heroism of which her ears will never hear !

Meanwhile the 15th Division, having captured the Lens Road Redoubt that straddled the Lens-Béthune road, were engaged in clearing the northern portion of the village of Loos. The 1st Division, the left wing of the Fourth Corps, had met with varying fortune. The 1st Brigade had penetrated to the enemy's reserve trenches in front of Cité St. Elie and Hulluch, roughly upon the line of the Lens-La Bassée road. The 2nd Brigade, impeded by a mass of concealed wire that our fire had failed to destroy, were held up in the direction of Lone Tree and Bois Carrée. This necessitated the bringing up of the divisional reserve, who managed to advance between the left flank of the 15th Division and the Loos Road Redoubt, a strong point in the German line on the track leading from Loos to Vermelles. This relieved the pressure on the 2nd Brigade, and the Loos Road Redoubt, attacked from the front and both flanks, fell into our hands, compelling some six or seven hundred of the enemy to surrender. But the delay had enabled the Germans to reinforce Hulluch and the Crassier of Puits XIII bis to such an extent that the attack was diverted to the right, in which direction it advanced as far as the Bois Hugo and Puits XIV bis, both being situated on the eastern slope of the valley to the north of Hill 70. Of the events of the afternoon it is impossible to speak with any degree of certainty. It seems most probable that the paths of the three divisions having brought them all on to the rising ground to the eastward and north-eastward of Loos, an attack was made upon the redoubt that existed on Hill 70 at the point where a track from Loos to Cité St. Auguste crosses the Lens-La Bassée road. It also seems probable that after many vicissitudes this redoubt was captured and subsequently held, though by a force utterly inadequate for the purpose. About 8 p.m. a messenger reached one of our batteries, having lost his way in the dark, bearing a message addressed to the headquarters of one of the Brigades forming the

15th Division, to the effect that the sender was holding Hill 70 with a mixed handful of men, numbering a thousand in all, and urgently requesting the immediate supply of sandbags and other material for defence.

In the battery we were, of course, ignorant of all these things at the time, and the progress of events could only be conjectured by the position of the spots upon which we were ordered to fire and the reports of wounded passing by us on their way to the rear. We knew of the fall of Loos by the forlorn procession of refugees who had been living in the village all through the German occupation, but who were sent back immediately upon the capture of the place by our troops. Be it noted in parenthesis that much consternation was caused in a certain office by the arrival of a telephone message to this effect : " The loose women are expected shortly, please arrange for their accommodation ! " From the observation post came the news of the taking of the Double Crassier and the Cemetery, but beyond that, and the information that no attack had been launched towards the Puits XVI ridge, the observing officer had nothing further to tell us. But I think that in the ominous absence of any further reference to our projected advance, we all felt something of the chill breath of disappointment, that whispered that our high hopes had somehow failed of their realization.

VI

STRAIGHTENING THE LINE

STRAIGHTENING out the line is an expression frequently found in official dispatches, and it may usually be understood to cover the operations that take place after a definite attack. In the case of the Battle of Loos, these operations extended into the third week of October, and as a corollary to an account of this great event, and as a study of what was in effect a series of minor battles, the following sketch is intended. There were many events during these days that are not yet fully understood, the time has not yet come when a dispassionate history may be written. Controversy is yet busy with the names of many disputed positions. I make no attempt at contribution to any opinion expressed, but merely endeavour to convey some faint idea of such portions of the drama as were played before the eyes of the artillery observers.

During the night of September 25–26,

the general position was something as
follows. The enemy, from a point not far
south of Fosse 8 to the Double Crassier, had
been driven out of his front line to a greater
or less distance in rear. Here, many months
before this time, he had already constructed
a second line of defence in anticipation of
such a possibility. We, finding ourselves
confronted by this line, were obliged to make
some sort of cover for our advanced infantry,
using the abandoned German front line and
communication trenches as far as they could
be adapted for our reserves and supports.
Along the whole of this front of advance,
therefore, both sides were busily engaged
upon strengthening their respective positions, covering meanwhile their working
parties with rifle fire. The artillery could
not render much direct assistance, the light
had failed before the final positions of the
infantry on either side were determined,
and the risk of injuring friends as much as
foes was too great. The function of the guns
was to keep a steady fire directed upon the
possible lines of approach of hostile reinforcements, which were pouring up on both
sides during the whole of the night. The
front of advance was something as follows :
From the south of the canal we remained in

G

our old trenches to a point just north of the quarries, and from here the position we held ran through the front line of the Hohenzollern Redoubt, of which we held the front and the enemy the rear, thence somewhat to the west of the Lens-La Bassée road in front of Cité St. Elie and Hulluch, through Chalk Pit Wood and Puits XIV bis, somewhere over the western slopes of Hill 70, then abruptly back to the Double Crassier, where it joined our old line again.

Up till midnight both sides worked comparatively undisturbed, except on Hill 70, where attacks and counter-attacks followed one another without intermission. But at about 12.30 a.m., the enemy, having apparently succeeded in bringing up sufficient troops for the purpose, made a series of local attacks, the fiercest of which seems to have been on our line from the Bois Hugo to Hill 70. This attack was repulsed, as were the remainder of the series made at the same time. The weather now became even more misty than before, and the cold drizzle that had been falling all the evening increased in intensity. Shortly after dawn, at 5.30 a.m., the enemy made a more determined attack from much the same part of his line, in which he scored some initial successes, afterwards retrieved, and by 6.30 a.m. the position was the same as it had been all night. Observation was extremely bad on the morning of the 26th, so much so that it was fully 8 a.m. before artillery could be effectively used. But at this hour we again assumed the offensive, and opened a furious bombardment upon the redoubt on the summit of Hill 70, a work already of extreme strength, and now doubly so after the feverish energies of large working parties during the night. At nine o'clock the bombardment ceased, and the infantry rushed to the assault, but were unable to penetrate the hostile defences. They were re-formed and the attempt was repeated, again unsuccessfully.

Towards mid-day the local offensive passed into the hands of the enemy, who made a determined attack from the Bois Hugo and succeeded in driving our line back a considerable distance and recapturing Puits XIV bis. This was a distinct advantage to him, for it gave him a point of vantage from which he could direct machine-gun fire upon the flank of troops moving to the assault of Hill 70. No further determined attacks were made by either side on the afternoon of the 26th or the night 26th–27th, although desultory fighting continued, and various reliefs and reinforcements were made amongst our own troops. The 3rd Cavalry Division, who up till now had been waiting for the chance that would have been theirs had we succeeded in piercing the German line, were dismounted and relieved the troops holding Loos, where they remained for a couple of days, some of them taking part in the final assault upon Hill 70 on the 27th.

On the afternoon of the 27th every gun that could possibly be brought to bear opened a furious fire upon the Hill 70 Redoubt. For two hours the bombardment continued in a light that nearly broke the observers' hearts, so early did the evening close in, and so persistently hung the mist. Then, with one earth-shaking salvo from the massed batteries, it ceased, and the Guards Division rushed to the assault. What they achieved will probably never be accurately known, undoubtedly they penetrated the first line of the redoubt, but the enemy, continually reinforced from his fortress of Cité St. Auguste, contrived to expel them, and slowly they were swept back, in the gathering darkness of night, to the positions from which they had sprung. The attack had failed, Hill 70, the key of Lens, was still in the enemy's hands.

The strength of this position lay perhaps not so much in its natural advantages, as in the artificial means which had been employed to render it capable of effective defence. Its position upon one of the main arteries leading from the fortress of Lens made it easy to reinforce from Cité St. Auguste, one of the outliers of that fortress. The western slopes of the hill, up which the attack must come, formed a sort of glacis to the redoubt, on to which observers in the redoubt itself or in the woods around La Ferme des Mines de Lens could direct fire from their batteries at Pont-a-Vendin, Cité St. Emile and Cité St. Laurent. The work itself was of considerable extent and exceptionally formidable, and was probably impregnable by frontal attack when fully manned. Further, all possible approaches to it were enfiladed from the northward by machine-gun fire from Puits XIV bis and some ruined houses at the edge of a small wood, and from the southward by the strong works at the edge of Cité St. Auguste, namely Puits XI and a building known as the Dynamitière. Our failure to capture this important strategical point was therefore regrettable, but not incomprehensible.

A couple of days after the failure of our last attack upon Hill 70, a redistribution of the front took place between the Allied Armies. The Tenth French Army took over the new line up to a point near the Chalk Pit Wood, the boundary of their territory, which included the village of Loos, being now roughly a line drawn from this point through Quality Street, and thence along the Lens-Béthune Road. From this time Hill 70 ceased to be a British objective, and the whole of the line in front of Lens came under one command, instead of being divided right in front of the fortress, a change of considerable administrative advantage.

During these days, from the 25th to the end of the month, there had been spasmodic fighting along the rest of the front of advance, especially about the quarries and the Hohenzollern Redoubt. This latter work, in which we had gained a footing on the 25th, was repeatedly reported lost and re-captured, but eventually it was found to be untenable under the enemy's fire from **Auchy** and **Fosse 8,** and to a lesser degree from **Cité St. Elie** and **Hulloch.** The actual new line as now consolidated was therefore the same as on the evening of the 25th, except that it ran to the westward of the Hohenzollern and at the foot of the slopes of Hill 70.

During the succeeding week no events of outstanding importance took place, the infantry were busy in the improvement of their new trenches, and the artillery in keeping the hostile batteries quiet while they did so. But on October 8, " the lid suddenly came off Hell," as Gunner Wolverhampton aptly expressed it. During the early part of the morning the enemy had been unusually quiet, but about ten o'clock he opened a bombardment upon the whole of the new line, more especially upon that part of it in front of Loos, upon the village itself, and upon the trenches between **Hill 70** and the **Double Crassier.** This bombardment grew in intensity, and towards noon we were ordered to retaliate upon certain parts of his line. A few minutes later, the wind being in his favour, he let loose a dense cloud of smoke and gas, and at the same time lifted his fire on to our batteries and

observation stations, employing a large percentage of lachrymatory gas shell. Very
shortly after this, his counter-attack was
launched. As on the 25th, very little was
visible from our observation stations, owing
to the obscurity caused by the smoke. It
appears, however, that he developed two
separate attacks, one issuing from the Bois
Hugo and the other from the directions of
the Dynamentière and Puits XI. These
attacking columns were composed of waves
of men in close order, each wave, according
to the French observers, who were more
suitably placed as far as noting details
went than our own, as the smoke did not
blow in their direction, being composed of
a mass of men six abreast and twenty-five
deep. The French field batteries were at
that time massed close together, and their
commander held their fire until the attackers
were well clear of the cover from which
they issued. As soon as this was the case,
every battery was ordered to open fire at its
maximum rate, which they did with results
that were nothing short of appalling. Our
battery happened to be just in front of them,
and anything like their fire cannot be
imagined. For fully an hour the continu-

ous roar was such that telephones were useless, orders shouted through a megaphone into the recipient's ear absolutely inaudible. The effect of such a cannonade upon a slow moving mass of men in the open may be imagined. It is said that the loss of one of the attacking columns in dead alone was upwards of six thousand, and this estimate was subsequently largely increased. The hopeless position of these unfortunates, was, curiously enough, enhanced by an accident. One French battery had suffered severely a few days before, having been badly shelled, whereby it had lost all its officers and had had to change its position. Being at this time still somewhat disorganized, it was late in opening fire, and when it did so, opened at the same range as the other batteries had done some minutes before, thereby directing its fire upon a point that the attackers had already passed over, so placing a curtain of fire behind them. Caught thus between two hail-storms of shell, the massed columns had no escape, and were mown down where they stood.

The conditions in the battery during this affair were curious and extremely interesting. Each gun was firing as fast as the shell

could be loaded and the round laid, orders
being passed by gesticulation as best they
could. Behind us the roar of the French
batteries grew until it was only by watching
for the flashes that we could tell when our
own guns had fired. All round the hostile
shells were bursting, filling the air with a
sweet ether-like vapour that sent a sharp
pain shooting through one's eyes until it
seemed as if complete blindness must shortly
supervene. The tears coursing down the
men's faces made strange white tracks
through the grime of battle, till the detachments became fierce, ghost-like and terrible,
the reeking demons of the pit, striving and
sweating that they might slay ever more and
more, that the bitter screams of their mutilated victims might swell ever louder into
the livid heavens. And the endless succession of ammunition wagons, their drivers
clad in gas-helmets till they resembled the
Inquisitors of old, lashing their horses into
a yet more frantic gallop as they neared
their goal, seemed as the shell burst all about
them like monstrous chariots of hell. And
all the time the French reserves were mass-
ing behind us, passing in turn down the
boyaux into the threatened trenches, each

party as they passed cheering the roaring guns, and winning from the detachments a hoarse shout in return, as for a moment they rested from their ceaseless labour.

Slowly the inferno of sound died away, and with its first ebb came the voice of rumour. We had lost the Double Crassier, and the enemy had gained a footing on the slag-heap of Fosse 5, he was close to us, and we should have to save the guns as best we could! The French had repelled the attack, and, following up their advantage, had swept into Lens! The truth of the affair we did not discover till later, when it appeared that a portion of our new line from the middle of the Double Crassier north-wards had been captured, re-occupied and captured again, that the enemy had been finally driven out, but that the trench was now so full of dead as to afford no cover to the living. But for this minor success, if success it was, the furious counter-attack had failed with great loss to the enemy. If our total losses during the operations of September and October were between eighty and ninety thousand, it is believed that the enemy lost about ten thousand upon this one day alone. During the night of the

8th–9th the Germans contrived to establish themselves in the disputed length of trench, but otherwise the position remained for the next two days the same as before the counter-attack.

On the 11th the French developed a fresh attack in this sector, with the primary object of retaking the lost trench, and the secondary object of pushing such successes they might achieve right up past the end of the Double Crassier and Puits XI until they should rest upon the mineral railway running past Puits XI and Cité St. Pierre as far as Cité St. Elisabeth, thus forming an offensive line from which to threaten the Dynamitière and the enemy's approaches to Hill 70. We were called upon to assist in this enterprise, and at 2 p.m. commenced to drop shell along the Lens-La Bassée and Lens-Béthune roads, from their junction in Lens up to Cité St. Auguste and Cité St. Laurent. We also kept the church in the latter place under fire to prevent its use as an observation station. About 3 p.m. the French launched their troops to the assault, and succeeded in recapturing the lost trench, but owing to intense machine-gun fire from Puits XI and XII and from Cité St. Pierre,

they failed to advance any further along the
line of the Double Crassier towards the
mineral railway.

The primary object of the operations so
far had been the capture of Lens. The
importance of the place can hardly be over-
estimated. If we imagine England with
Lancashire and the West Riding in hostile
occupation, we shall have a parallel to the
case of France deprived of the Department
du Nord and part of Pas de Calais, except
that in our own case we should still have
left to us many manufacturing districts,
and France has but few. The importance
to the economic life of France of the three
towns of Lille, Roubaix and Tourcoing is
comparable to the importance of Manchester
to us, and the coal-mining districts lying
round Lens, which include such fields as
those of Courrières, Drocourt and Dourges
occupy relatively a far more important
position than those of the West Riding.
Lens itself is the key to this productive
area, whose energies are at least as valuable
to the enemy as to its rightful owners, and
Lens has in skilful hands become a fortress
in the modern sense, far more difficult of
capture than older works at one time deemed

impregnable. It is comparatively easy to concentrate fire upon guns whose position is known, as they must be when permanently mounted in the fortifications of the text-books, and once a sufficient concentration of fire has been obtained, guns so sited, being incapable of removal, must sooner or later be put out of action, but it is impossible so utterly to destroy a city and its suburbs that its ruins are no longer sufficient to afford cover to mobile ordnance and machine guns. It has been found that a building that in itself is merely a screen from direct observation, becomes, when destroyed by artillery fire, a heap of ruins amongst which may be concealed artillery and machine guns, and which by its very mass is an excellent protection against hostile fire. Bombard this type of fortress as you will, its defenders are not tied by their gun-mountings to any one position, but can move their batteries from place to place, knowing full well that the attackers, with each round they fire, are preparing fresh situations wherein they may be concealed. It will surely be found that this war has sounded the knell of permanently fixed guns except for purposes of coast defence, where alone the immobile gun has triumphed in the face of many years' accumulation of scornful criticism.

The last phase of the operations was due to a desire on our part to strengthen as much as possible our position from the quarries to the new point of junction with the French. On October 13 our battery was ordered to open a bombardment upon the German trenches that lay along the Lens-La Bassée road to the west of Hulluch. This bombardment continued for an hour or so, and at two o'clock the infantry advanced to the assault, we at the same time lifting our fire on to the village of Hulluch itself, starting at the western end and slowly increasing the range so as gradually to drive through the whole place. But at half-past three our hopes of a capture of Hulluch similar to that of Loos were dashed to the ground by an order from headquarters to come back on to the western edge of the village. This we did until darkness supervened, and we were ordered to cease firing. As far as we were concerned, this was the most exacting day we had yet known, our expenditure of ammunition during the five or six hours that we were in action being greater than that of any previous day. So rapidly were the guns worked that the continual concussion broke the platform of one of the guns, so that in the middle of the action it had to be hauled out of its pit on to a hard road close by, and fired without concealment of any kind, regardless of the risk of observation from hostile captive balloons or aeroplanes. It may be added that next day the detachment found some rafters in a ruined building and from these constructed a new platform for themselves without any form of skilled assistance.

It was not until the next day that we learnt the history of the attack. The intention had been to capture the Hohenzollern Redoubt, and from that as a *point d'appui* to extend our line along the Lens-La Bassée road as far as Chalk Pit Wood, with the possibility of capturing Cité St. Elie and Hulluch as advance posts. The attempt only partially succeeded. We contrived to advance our line in front of Hulluch almost on to the road, but failed to occupy permanently any of the German trenches. The Hohenzollern was apparently taken, but could not be held, as upon September 25, under concentrated fire from Fosse 8. Between Cité St. Elie and Hulluch, also, history re-

peated itself. Concealed wire, so placed
that the artillery observers could find no
place from which satisfactorily to observe
the effect of their fire, held up the infantry
assault. An attempt had been made to
destroy this wire by map shooting combined
with the use of high-explosive shell, but the
destruction was not complete, and the attack
failed. It was said that a handful of men
actually penetrated into Hulluch but were
never seen again, and that for a short time
our infantry held the German trenches in
front of the village. But with the enemy
established in houses overlooking them, and
occupying a strong commanding line along
the crassier of Puits XIII bis, these trenches
were untenable and had to be evacuated.
The net gain of ground during the day was
a depth of some two hundred yards on a
front of rather less than a mile. At the same
time the French, who had been supporting
our attack upon the right, reported that the
northern suburbs of Lens, Cités St. Auguste,
St. Laurent and St. Pierre, had been so
carefully prepared and were held in such
strength that for the moment a frontal
attack upon them was inadvisable.

Here, then, the offensive operations that

H

began with the Four Days' bombardment,
may be said to have ended.   Although the
gain of ground seemed insignificant, consisting as it did of one ruined village and a few
square miles of fallowland, and although
Lens still stood triumphant and untaken,
there is still much to be reckoned in the
Allies' favour.   Victory it was not, and no
amount of advertisement will ever make
it so.   But it was an exhibition of strength
on the part of the Allies, and a stern re-
minder to the enemy that their power of
offensive on the Western Front had permanently passed into our hands.   The resources
in men, money and munitions of the Central
Powers are decreasing, those of the Allies
increasing; equal losses on either side, therefore, is a condition favourable to the latter.
It is maintained that our losses were too
great in proportion to the results achieved.
Yes, perhaps they were, but, had they been
only slightly greater, had more men been
flung into the struggle at the critical time,
it is impossible to forecast what the issue
of the fighting might have been.   The enemy
knew this, and was prepared for a substantial retirement.   Conjecture is unprofitable, but let us as a nation learn the lesson

that men and men alone will terminate this
war. Other factors may check it tempor-
arily; it may be to the advantage of the
enemy to agree to an apparently disastrous
peace in order to gain a respite for fresh
preparation. But a certain page of history
should harden our resolution, should make
us convinced of the bitter fact that there is
no peace for the world except in the disappearance of the German Empire or our
own. *Delenda est Carthago*—let us preach
the lessons of the Punic wars in season and
out of season till every soul in these islands
realizes their significance at the present day.
The world is no larger than it was then, there
is still no room in it for two rival World
Powers, one must sink into obscurity before
the might of its rival.   And, accepting this in-
controvertible fact as an axiom, let us face our
position, let us remember how the power of
Rome trembled in the balance as she strained
every nerve in her system during Hannibal's
Italian campaign, and let us realize at last
that the destruction of our rival will demand
of us sacrifices compared to which the
efforts that we have yet made are nothing,
are as the puny efforts of a feeble infant
contrasted with the struggle of a strong man

wrestling for his life.   And if the operations that have been named the Battle of Loos have any share in bringing these things home to us, their effects will be far more beneficial than those of a spectacular victory.

VII

LOOS

ONE of our officers was fortunate enough, very shortly after the events of September 25, to have the opportunity of reconnoitring the village of Loos, with a double purpose in view, namely to verify some landmarks that were doubtful from our observation posts, and to discover if any points existed suitable for permanent occupation as O.Ps. There were two ways open to him of reaching the village from his battery position, of which the first was to proceed to North Maroc and thence take the road to Les Cabarets and from there the track that runs into Loos at its south-western corner, and the second was to walk to Quality Street, thence along the Lens-Béthune road to the old German front-line, and so through their communication trenches into any required part of the village. Time being of importance, he chose the former method, and set out one morning at about 8 a.m. The narrative of his adventures in Loos, as throwing light upon the conditions obtaining in a place that had been heavily shelled by us until our capture of it, and has ever since been equally heavily shelled by the enemy, may be of some interest.

Once clear of the houses that screened his movements from the hostile lines, the road seemed very lonely and deserted. So far as the eye could see he was the only living person in the whole of the wide valley, and the sense of being under the observation of many pairs of eyes that were to him invisible produced in him a strangely nervous reaction, as though he were the principal actor in some horrible nightmare. It seemed as though every footstep rang upon the hard road with a note audible for miles, as though he were a gigantic black figure upon an unbroken background of white, as though the watching eyes bent such burning rays upon him that he could feel them pierce him as he moved. I have walked that road myself many times since, more than once when it has been under fire, and know now that it is as safe or safer than many others whose dangers never concern the most nervous, yet an echo of these first sensations of his has invariably struck

me when I have done so, and I can understand his feelings. It can only be attributed
to the fact that being alone in the middle of
the valley one imagines that one is a conspicuous target for any one who will to spend
a round upon.

The road crosses first our own old front
line, then the German, over both of which
substantial bridges had been built directly
after the advance. It was not until he had
crossed our own line that the cost of the
battle became evident to him. Then he
began to understand. Between the lines
a burial party was at work, busy with the
task of identifying and interring our own
dead. Behind the German line the operation
of clearing the battlefield had scarcely begun. Here the dead lay thick, our own and
the enemy's in inextricable confusion. Here
was a group of three or four, showing where a
well-timed shrapnel had burst, there four or
five in a line, stricken down as they charged
by rifle fire from some fiercely-held support
trench. And everywhere, mingling with the
dead, were all the many insignia of war,
rifles, ammunition, tins of beef, biscuits,
cases of bombs, some unopened, some with
their contents scattered round them, everything that is carried forward in a modern

battle. At Les Cabarets itself, which is in reality the junction of the Lens-Béthune and Grenay-Hulluch roads, and which lies a few hundred yards south-east of the Lens Road Redoubt, the struggle seemed to have been fiercer. It is probable that the ruins of the houses that once stood at the cross-road had been held by a detachment of the enemy, for lying round them were a heap of dead Germans, their rifles in many cases still in their hands, and about these in a narrow circle the bodies of our attacking troops, some lying as they had fired, their legs spread out, their rifles fallen from their shoulders and their heads resting on them, as though an angel of sleep had touched them even as they pulled the trigger. Close by, two horses bearing the brand of the broad arrow were quietly grazing on the rank grass that covered the fallow land, their broken harness still hanging on their backs, evidently the team of a shell-shattered wagon that lay near by. My friend was tempted to pause and investigate further, but a dozen bullets whizzing by quickly convinced him that the locality was not healthy, and he made haste upon his way. Nor was he more lucky with the track that led from here towards Loos. Some persevering sniper

evidently regarded him as fair game, and
after this enthusiast had displayed his mark-
manship by narrowly missing him twice in
quick succession, my friend abandoned the
field to him and took to a communication
trench that ran in the required direction.
He says that he hopes never to take a more
hideous walk. The trench was literally
paved with dead Germans—it must have
been used as a line of defence against the
advance of the 47th Division—some lying
on their backs with their eyes staring heaven-
wards, others horribly buried in the thick
clay that lay in the lower stretches of the
trench, so that his attention was only called
to their presence by a sudden dreadful yield-
ing beneath his feet. They lay too thick
for it to be possible to avoid treading upon
them, and though more than once he deserted
the trench for the clean earth of the plains,
his friend the sniper was bent on each occasion upon showing him that he was still a
happy memory to him, and he was forced
to descend again. However, it was over at
last, and with the greatest relief that he had
ever experienced he found himself in the
shelter of the outlying houses of Loos.

Here for a few minutes he stood and studied
a plan with which he had been provided.

His objective was the Pylons, easy enough to see, certainly, but unfortunately on the far side of an open square or market-place by the church, upon which the German gunners were making very pretty practice with field guns and light howitzers. There was nothing for it but to find a way round, along the streets choked with rubbish and torn by great craters, taking short cuts through gardens converted into cemeteries, in which the dead lying on the surface were more numerous than those below, across courtyards wherein the horses who had been stabled there lay where the flying bullets had found them. Strange work, this threading of the city of the dead, the sense of isolation growing as one advanced until one seemed a visitant to a world struck by a celestial bombardment that had left none alive to tell the tale. Troops there were in plenty, but they remained in the wonderful excavations that had been made; none, save rarely a messenger, crouching behind a wall as the whizz and roar of the shell echoed amongst the torn buildings, racing across an open space in a brief interval of quiet, ventured forth, unless before dawn to relieve his companions who were stationed in the hastily-dug trenches in front of the

village. But during the course of this expedition my friend discovered a very valuable
fact, namely, that the principal fire of the
enemy was directed only upon certain spots,
and was not being distributed indiscriminately over the village. Avoid these spots,
and except for a few casual " universal "
bursting overhead, one was perfectly safe,
voilà tout! But that same casual universal
is a very jumpy toy. You hear it coming,
certainly, but far too quickly for you to
do anything, and before you know where
you are it has burst just over you with an
ear-splittting crack, and small fragments
hit the ground all round you with a most
unpleasant thud. " Woolly bears," the
men call them, for they leave a curious
cotton-wool-like wreath of smoke in the air
for some seconds, much larger and more
lasting than the puff of a shrapnel.

Very shortly after this first discovery,
my friend made another, which somewhat
counterbalanced his relief in the first, which
was that one of the points most distinctly
to be avoided was the very place he wished
to reach, the Pylons themselves. Round
about their base a howitzer battery was
methodically placing high-explosive shell,
and amongst the upper works a field battery

was making very accurate practice with
those most undesirable " woolly bears."
There was nothing for it, however, and the
longer one stopped and looked at it the
worse it seemed, so, with feelings utterly
unlike those that are popularly supposed to
steel the heart of the hero who boldly faces
death for his country's sake, he made his
way under cover of such houses as still
remained, to the mine buildings at the foot
of the great steel structure. Here was destruction such as he had never seen. The
buildings, strongly as they had been built
to withstand the weight of the machinery
within them, were completely shattered,
their contents strewing the floors like scrap
iron in a merchant's yard. Great iron girders
were cut as by a knife, the bridge leading
from the Pylons to the loading stages on the
end of the Crassier, a riveted steel structure,
was broken in half, the ends torn and frayed
as though made of paper. The towers
themselves are so massive and their weight
is so distributed among many uprights, that,
although many of these latter were bent or
broken, the edifice they supported still stood
gaunt and menacing, dominating the countryside. But their foot was no place to sit in
idle conjecture that morning, as a shell that

nearly blocked up the entrance to the shelter
into which he had made his way abruptly
reminded him. Waiting until its last fragments had fallen—a process that takes a
surprisingly long time—he made a bolt over
the ruins, climbing and scrambling up a
refuse-covered slope, until he reached the
foot of the winding stairs that rose up the
centre of one of the towers. Fortunately
for him, this stairway was partly enclosed
by sheets of boiler-plate, for the next shell
burst uncomfortably close and the fragments
hit the boiler-plate with a sound that left
no doubt in his mind of what his fate would
have been had this shield not been there.
Up the spiral stairway then—was ever
such an interminable flight? Surely, notwithstanding the friendly morning mist, the
whole German army must see him as he
climbed ever higher! Those friendly steel
sheets had been hit direct more than once
at various times, leaving several turns of the
stairway open, plain to everybody's view.
However, nothing alarming happened, and
the goal was reached—not the top of the
tower where the winding pulleys hung, but a
gallery that had formed the upper limit of
travel of the cage, where the trolleys were
unloaded and pushed across the bridge to

the loading sheds.   This gallery or platform
stood perhaps a hundred and fifty feet above
the ground, and had once been glazed, but
long ago every pane of glass had been
shattered and the steel floor was thickly
carpeted with the fragments.   Once in the
gallery one was fairly safe, for the floor and
roof were of steel and so was the circular
wall up to the level of the glazing.   Nothing
but pieces of shell coming through the
windows—and the place was full of fragments
showing where this had happened—or a
direct hit from a heavy shell could do much
damage.   But it was not the place for a
rest-cure, the moral effect of " woolly bears "
bursting amongst the girder-work close to
one, although one knew that by the time
one heard the report the danger was over,
was most disturbing.   Once, too, a fairly
heavy shell hit the tower itself, causing it to
rock like a sapling in a gale, as my friend
expressed it afterwards.   His first thought
was of the delights of his situation had it
carried away part of the staircase, when he
would be faced by the prospect of staying
where he was till dusk or of swarming down
the steelwork in full view of the German
trenches, but fortunately this contingency did
not arise.

But the view that he obtained amply
compensated for everything. From the
grim black mass of Fosse 8, past the tower
of Cité St. Elie, the cupola of Douvrin, the
trees, magnificent in their thick verdure, that
clothe the banks of a little stream that flows
past Hulluch, to the strange medley of
chimneys and elevators that gives to the
works of the Société Metallurgique de Pont-
à-Vendin the appearance of a fore-and-aft
rigged vessel under sail, the whole country
lay spread as on a map.   Further south still,
Lens and its thickly-built suburbs could be
seen, and towards the west, the well-known
country that we held, the high land of the
Vimy Ridge, with Souchez at its feet, the
tall slag-heaps of Noeux-les-Mines and Auchel,
the dark mass of the Bois des Dames, the
square tower of Béthune.   What an observation post ! No wonder that the enemy,
whose use of the place for that very purpose
was apparent by the presence of German
newspapers and a broken table with some
scraps of paper upon it, were determined to
make it untenable by constant shelling.

For utterly impossible as a permanent
observation post it undoubtedly was, and
my friend, having verified his geography,
left it with a feeling of deep thankfulness

at having escaped unhurt. But his adventures were by no means at an end, he had still to find a situation of comparative safety from which he could observe when required under more restful conditions. The first place he selected was a house in the Enclosure, as the buildings near the foot of the Pylons have been termed. This also had been used by the enemy for the same purpose, for the walls were sandbagged, the lower floors were shored up with pit-props, and the basement had evidently been occupied by a fairly large party. Curiously enough, the house was in quite good repair, the walls and half the roof were standing, in contrast to the wreckage that lay around it. Here the explorer received what he describes as " the shock of his life," for on opening the door of one of the upper rooms he found, sprawling over a table as though just fallen asleep, the body of a German officer, still holding a pencil with which he had been addressing a post-card to a girl in Magdeburg. So lifelike was the attitude that it was impossible to realize at first that he was dead, notwithstanding the jagged hole above the temple where the fragment had entered and the blood that stained his right side. From this room a good view of the desired

stretch of country could be obtained, there
was a plentiful supply of sandbags ready
filled in the house, and it seemed in every
way desirable. But, just as my friend had
determined upon converting it to his own
uses, a (fortunately) small shell, evidently
intended for the Pylons, but a little "over,"
entered the ground floor and burst there,
wrecking the staircase, bringing down ceil-
ings and tiles all over the house and smashing
what was probably the last pane of glass in
Loos. If this place was going to play long-
stop for all the byes that passed the Pylons,
it was distinctly unhealthy. He clambered
down the wreckage of the stairs and looked
round for a more likely spot, settling upon
a tall house some little distance away. But
here again he was doomed to disappointment.
As he walked towards it a light howitzer
shell sang over his head and burst a hundred
yards beyond his goal. Instinct told him
that this was the first round of a series of
which his projected O.P. was the target.
Even as he realized that he was standing
about the same distance short of the place
as the first round had fallen over, and in a
direct line, the second shell passed so close
to him that he swears he felt the wind of it,
and burst in a manure-heap not ten yards

I

away. Thanking heaven that it had found
a soft billet that muffled the force of its
explosion, he turned and bolted, having no
further interest in observing that particular
series, the components of the manure-heap
dropping in a shower about him.

The next place he came to was a biggish
building in a part of the town that seemed
to be immune from shelling. He walked
boldly into it and climbed up to an attic in
the roof. Here were more signs of German
occupation, a window that faced towards
our old line being heavily sandbagged, whilst
behind it was a neatly constructed platform
and rest. Hundreds of empty cartridge-
cases scattered over the floor and a few
loaded clips still lying on the platform
showed that the sniper whose lair it had been
had known good sport there. But even here
my friend was not destined to rest undisturbed. Hardly had his eye taken in these
details than a sound of hurried whispers
below burst upon his ears, and a peremptory voice bade him " Descendez, vite ! "
" Qu'est-ce qu'il-y-a ? " he replied. " Descendez, vite, vite, ou nous allons tirer ! "
Discretion was by far the better part of
valour, so down he came, to be surrounded

at once by a number of French soldiers
armed with rifles and fixed bayonets. To
his enquiries as to what they wanted, the
only reply was, " Vous pouvez dire ce que
vous voulez à M. le Commandant." The
latter gentleman was very comfortably installed in a roomy cellar, and my friend was
ushered into his presence with the significant
words, " C'est un espion que nous avons
attrappé en haut, mon Commandant, re-
gardez ces machines-là qu'il porte ! " The
latter presumably in reference to the sextant,
compass and other strange-looking impedi-
menta that he carried. It was an uncom-
fortable moment, but he managed to establish his identity, and mutual explanations
followed, to the satisfaction of all parties,
and my friend was told that he might make
himself free of the place whenever he liked—
" Mais, monsieur, je crains que vous avez
trouvé en Loos que les français sont plus
dangereux que les allemands. Mais, peste,
vous êtes vraiment monté dans les Pylons !
J'ôse bien dire, comme disent les Anglais,
que c'état un endroit ' not sanitary ' ! " As
a variant upon the hackneyed phrase " not
healthy," I think that this is hard to beat.

The next question was the best way of

getting home. The friendly mist had by now disappeared, and it was hardly advisable to face the open road again, even if this had not involved the ghastly walk along the death-strewn communication trench. My friend finally decided to find the end of a communication trench that, starting from a point in the north-western corner of the village, led into the old German front line between the Lens Road and the Loos Road Redoubts. To reach this the greater part of Loos had to be traversed, but the streets in this direction were fairly safe. They were, however, even more encumbered with the dead bodies of men and horses than those in the other half of the town. It seems that a large number of men had been driven to the dug-outs and bombed there, and that when these same dug-outs were required for Allied occupation, their former tenants were evicted into the road, for the burial parties to deal with when time permitted. Wonderful structures were these dug-outs, examples of the enemy's thoroughness. Not content with the protection afforded by a cellar, in many places they had excavated large chambers below the cellars themselves, whose floors they had paved with bricks and whose

walls they had lined with boards.   Once in
them the garrison was perfectly safe from
the most furious bombardment.

A further example of method was to be
seen in the treatment of shells that had fallen
blind. When these were of medium size,
they had been collected in small heaps and
surrounded with barbed wire to prevent
inquisitive fingers experimenting with them.
In the back yard of a cottage lay the enormous bulk of a fifteen-inch shell, that had
judiciously been left where it fell, and had
been honoured by a complicated stockade of
its own. All this seemed to contrast with the
present state of the town, which was everywhere littered with military stores of every
conceivable kind. Some attempt had been
made to collect them into heaps, but even this
attempt had been very half-hearted. War
is, anyhow, an expensive amusement, and it
seems a pity to make it more so by sheer lack
of method. For not only Loos itself, but the
whole of the country over which the advance
was made was littered with arms, ammunition, equipment, bombs, in prodigious
numbers. My friend, having occasion to go
into Loos again some weeks later, found
these heaps still untouched, and was foolish

enough to report their existence and th
exact position. As a reward for this unw
ranted officiousness, he was requested
escort a wagon to Loos and indicate
localities where these various stores lay,
an evening when the battery was at
busiest, an invitation that he firmly declin

The way home, although much lon₉
proved to be cleaner and more secure,
sides having the interest of leading thro₁
the old German front line. This was t:
in the occupation of our reserves, and]
consequently been considerably tidied
but large parts of it were still comple₁
broken down, showing the effect of
bombardment. The shooting had b
distinctly good, very few shell-craters v
far from the trenches, and a large pro]
tion of the projectiles had either fallen i
them or blown in the parapet. But]
again the dug-outs must have afforded ₁
excellent protection. Wide shafts, dri
straight down from the front wall of
trench at an angle of forty-five degrees ₁
the horizontal, led into hollowed-out cham
twenty feet below the surface that w₁
easily accommodate a couple of dozen r
Each dug-out had more than one shaft

reduce the chances of men being buried by an explosion filling in the only means of exit. The trenches were everywhere revetted with timber or hurdles, and had a false bottom of wooden gratings to keep the men's feet as dry as possible. If only from the point of view of comfort they contrasted very favourably with our own, through which the homeward track next lay.

Loos, City of the Dead! If in years to come you are ever rebuilt, a task that to the observer of your utter destruction and desolation seems impossible, what strange and gruesome relics will your workmen find! Surely the Spirit of Carnage will for ever haunt those narrow streets and open widespread fields, surely your inhabitants of the future will wake in terror in the September nights to hear ghostly echoes of the then-forgotten struggle, the unceasing whistle and roar of the shells, the rushing footsteps of the charging men, the despairing cries of the bombed wretches in the cellars! And if timid eyes dare lift the curtain to peep fearfully through the windows, will they not see a blood-red moon shining upon streets through which pour the serried columns of the victors, and scent the night air tainted

with a faint sickening odour of slaughter?
But not alone shall Loos bear its burden of
horror, for in how many towns and villages
must these scenes be repeated befcre Peace
comes again !

VIII

IN FRENCH TERRITORY

At the beginning of October our battery, owing to reasons of strategy and convenience, changed its position by a matter of about a mile-and-a-half, and by so doing entered an area where the right of the British line joined the left of the French line. The actual point of junction of the lines varies from time to time, as much owing to the two armies' requirements in the matter of billets as for any other reason, and, as it happened, on the very day we moved into our new position, this point was in process of being moved a mile or so northwards. We saw, therefore, the familiar khaki give place to the looped-up blue greatcoat, and when, the desperate struggle to get the battery in order in the minimum time being over, we had time to look round and take note of our surroundings, we found ourselves in French Territory.

I think that the weeks we spent there were the happiest we have ever known, although the life of a gunner is a rough paradise for a man with health and strength —plenty of work, plenty of sport, and complete freedom from the cares of an artificial existence, there being nothing artificial about war. Our position was amongst ruined *corons*, not so badly damaged but that they could with very little trouble be made into very comfortable billets, and owing to the fact that it was in French territory, was immune from the visits of predatory "brass hats." Further, in our group commander we had a strong buckler against interference and aggression, and one in whom we all placed implicit confidence. His kindness to us all will be amongst the most precious memories of those happy days.

We found the change of tenants in the villages round us extremely advantageous in many ways, not the least of which was the amount of loot we acquired. It seems curious that the British Army, equipped as it is with a more copious transport than has ever before been imagined, should invariably leave in its wake enormous quantities of perfectly serviceable stores.

On this particular occasion we found abandoned more than enough overcoats and waterproof capes to fit out the whole battery, and collected from the billets into which we moved over a hundred thousand rounds of small-arm ammunition alone. Although these matters were reported, no steps were ever taken to remove the stores, and subsequent discoveries of hundreds of boxes of unused bombs met with the same indifference. What wonder that the thrifty French regard it as the best fortune that can befall them to take over any part of our line, or that French officers to whom I have spoken are inclined to base their opinions of our conduct of the war upon such indications of our national habits. " No army before has ever wasted as you waste," said one to me; " the food you reject would feed half the French Forces, the rifles you failed to collect after Loos would equip many battalions of your New Army. What is your proverb—' Straws show which way the wind blows '—is it not ? " Nor did the British troops leave only stores behind in their evacuation. Two days after the exchange, an officer arrived in the battery with a strange tale of woe. He was in command of a picquet

in a certain village, from where he had
watched his own people depart and the
French arrive, expecting every moment to
be relieved. Since that time he had received neither orders nor rations, and he
and his men had lived upon the charity
of a French regiment. We fed him and
sent him back to his lonely vigil with an
armful of provisions and a promise to report
his troubles through our headquarters. I
heard subsequently that his patrol had
been forgotten and never missed, so presumably he might have been there now
but for his own action.

The first and greatest Commandment
when on active service is this, " Thou shalt
covet thy neighbour's goods, and if he
doesn't keep his eye on them, thou shalt
possess them." Nationality seems to have
no effect upon the speed with which the
soldier assimilates this doctrine. The French
piou-piou is as great a follower of it as the
British Tommy, but his native politeness
lends to the act a more distinguished air.
Of course, British troops with their wasteful
ways are to him lawful game, and the first
couple of days in his company taught our
people habits of carefulness that were
never learnt before. Our most experienced

marauders returned empty-handed from raids
into the French lines, and this bred a respect
for our Allies that rapidly blossomed into
genuine friendship. And undoubtedly the
French soldier, taking him all round, is a
most charming person and an almost perfect
fighting man. He takes life very seriously,
and is frequently scandalized by our behaviour, not quite understanding that a
mask of frivolity may be only the result
of a desire to make light of difficulties and
to hearten others, hiding in reality an
immovable determination to do one's duty.
" Pour vous, la guerre n'est pas sérieuse,"
said a big Breton to me once, and I,
knowing the melancholy tendencies of his
race, knew not what to reply. But next
day a party of which he formed one, doubled
past the battery. " Que faites-vous ? " I
called as he passed. With a face wreathed
in smiles he replied, " Nous allons donner
aux Bosches un petit coup de fusil, ça sera
très amusant, hein ? "

Of the picturesque appearance of these
French troops a few words may be said.
There is an entry in my diary about this
time, " Walked down to headquarters this
morning. Saw two Frenchmen dressed
alike." And to the eyes of those accus-

tomed to unvarying khaki, the extraordinary
kaleidoscopic effect of steel helmet, képi,
coats of all conceivable colours, breeches
and trousers likewise, putties that shame
the rainbow, and an increasing note of
khaki with a dash of colour on the collar
or sleeve, strikes very strangely. Even the
men of the same regiment do not seem
to wear the same kit. One will be met
in steel helmet, dark blue coat and red
trousers, the next in képi, light blue coat
and breeches, and grass-green putties. The
authorities knew better than to waste the
stocks of clothing that they already had on
hand.

It would be impertinent to discuss the
fighting qualities of these superb troops.
The English Tommy, invariably a keen
and usually a perspicacious critic of everything that comes into his range of vision,
is apt to comment unfavourably upon what
appears to his eye as an undisciplined
mob strolling along the roads. But his
eyes are gradually opened as first of all
he discovers that these men, laden with a
far greater weight than he is ever called
upon to carry, are travelling quite as fast
as he cares to, and then, at the end of
the day, he finds that they have made them-

selves thoroughly comfortable and are enjoying a good meal long before he has thought of anything but the contents of his water-bottle. After that the revelation of their fighting qualities does not come as such a shock to him. Who that has seen them at work, for instance round Souchez or in their magnificent attack on the Double Crassier on October 11, can refrain from blessing our historic national luck for the Allies it has brought us?

And throughout his nature runs the Frenchman's traditional love for the turning of an honest penny. No sooner were we settled in our position than a bearded French soldier, probably a newsvendor in civil life, saw his golden opportunity. In his hours off duty he used to walk back many miles from the position, and return with an armful of English newspapers of the day before. How he procured them was a mystery we never solved, for he always arrived with them hours before we could obtain them anywhere ourselves. " Délé peppers ! " he would cry, and the whole battery turned out as one man to greet him and buy his wares, which, by the way, he sold cheaper than their price in the neighbouring towns. How much English he understood I never knew; he would talk it freely with the men, but never with the officers—" Non compris " and a shake of the head was his invariable reply to our advances in this direction. But he always knew the contents of the papers he sold, especially the *Daily Mail*. Certainly his ideas occasionally got a little mixed. I am convinced, for instance, that he was under the impression that Lord North-cliffe was either Dictator of England or had changed places with Lord Kitchener. "Monsieur Lor' Notcliffe il va bien ce matin ! " he would say with great satis-faction, " il va finir la guerre sur-le-champ." His politics swayed him to the extent that he always refused to bring us French dailies. "Mais non, je vous dis, monsieur. Vous aimez les journaux français ? Bien, demain je vous apporterai peut-être *La Vie Parisi-enne*, *Le Rire*, ce que vous voulez. Mais *Le Temps*, *Le Matin ?* Ceux sont les organes honteuses des capitalistes. *L'Homme Enchainé*, si vous voulez——"

He or one of his assistants (for it always seemed to me that half the French Army helped to carry his papers round for him) it was that first introduced us to the fascinations of the ring-making industry. It appears that an industrious Frenchman,

one supposes a jeweller by trade, early in
the war hit upon the idea of collecting the
fuses of hostile shells that fell near him,
melting down the aluminium of which they
are largely made, and casting it into rings,
which he ornamented by letting in pieces
of brass or copper, also components of the
fuse. The practice spread like wildfire
through the French troops, it gave a con-
genial occupation to their busy fingers, and
brought them a gratifying increase of in-
come. Our men were at first ready custo-
mers—there was little enough for them to
spend money upon, the inhabitants had
been cleared out of the surrounding villages, and no civilian population means no
estaminets. But some of the more com-
mercially-minded among us—the whole story
is as a microcosm of our commercial suprem-
acy as a nation—loath to see this profitable
trade passing them by, determined to enter
into competition. The first experiments
were dramatic enough. A band of telephonists collected a large store of wood torn
from ruined houses, and of coal, fetched at
no small risk from a mine that was usually
under fire, in the observation post, which
happened then to be a fairly large house
well back from the hostile lines, so that a

K

fire was allowed in the telephonists' room.
Here one evening they collected, like a band
of alchemists for the fusion of the Philosopher's Stone, and here I chanced upon them,
the room lit only by the glare of a huge fire,
around which they all crouched, their eyes
fixed upon a saucepan that held in its depths
one small fuse, which the Master of the
Black Arts periodically poked enquiringly
with the point of his bayonet. I believe
that attempt ended in the necessity for
a sudden and disastrous quenching, brought
about by the fact that the house itself
showed ominous signs of catching fire.
After many vicissitudes the art became
centred in the battery cooks, who, having
the unfair advantage that in the natural
course of events they worked by a fire all
day, formed a sort of Guild of Ring Makers,
and some very creditable work was produced.
Their first step was to undersell the French,
and they succeeded to such an extent that
the cook-house became a miniature Bir-
mingham, and orders had to be placed early
to secure delivery. Souvenirs these rings
became in a land where everybody seems
to ask everybody else for a " souvenir," a
term that has become so wide that it covers
everything portable. One day I was stand-

ing in a doorway when surely the youngest
soldier in the French army—he could not
have been more than fourteen; I suppose
he was a drummer boy, but how he reached
so close to the firing line has always puzzled
me—passed me and saluted gravely. My
smile must have reassured him, for he stopped
and after some hesitation looked at me
and saluted again. " Souvenir, monsieur ! "
he blurted out at last. " Souvenir ? " said
I, " Quelle espèce de souvenir désirez-vous ? "
With a grin that threatened to sever the
top of his head from the rest of his body,
he replied, " Souvenir de bully-beef, monsieur ! " He got it.

The flies that marred the soothing oint-
ment of this position were certain mysterious
bullets that flew about at strange hours of
the night and day. Nobody was ever
actually hit, but people strolling about
between the guns heard a whirr overhead
that made then duck involuntarily, and
heated officers would dash into the mess
swearing that they had seen bullets flatten
themselves against brick walls within an
inch of their noses. Scepticism, or even
a suggestion that they were spent bullets
from the firing line, was treated as insub-
ordination. A sniper it must be, a snark

who crept into our lines, shot his bolt, then softly and silently vanished away. One evening the combined patience of the battery could bear it no longer—I think somebody had staggered into the mess in a condition of collapse, and upon being revived with a rum ration, proceeded to explain how his cigarette had been shot out of his mouth by a bullet that passed between his teeth. At all events, it was decided to inform the French and request them to take steps to abate the nuisance. They, in the expressive jargon of the day, were all over it. Parties of men from their lines and our own crept out in the dusk to hunt the sniper—what a glorious opportunity of winning fame by returning with his scalp, or one of his ears, or whatever part of a sniper one does bring back as a trophy! Dozens of parties, each more subtle than the other in their proposed methods of action, crept out in the rapidly-falling dusk, and with them the greater number of our officers, armed with looted rifles and more subtlety than all the rest of the parties put together. Then night fell dark and moonless, and the fun began. Each party, busily engaged in its own game of blind-man's-buff, caught sight of some other party, and opened a hot and furious fire upon them. The remaining parties, seeing the flashes, emptied their magazines in their direction. By an hour or so after dark, the battle was in full swing. At ten o'clock such of the battery as were not engaged in the chase were cowering in their dug-outs and there was not a whole pane of glass for miles around. At half-past ten, a telephonist going to the O.P. to relieve his comrade was forced to take shelter in a disused communication trench, and to remain there all night, any attempt on his part to climb out being met by rapid fire from every direction at once. At eleven, a mitrailleuse was dragged up by an excited knot of men, and opened fire in the direction from which there seemed to come most noise. At half-past, fire had become general all along the line, everybody, supposing that his neighbour knew what he was aiming at, firing in the same direction as he did. At midnight the Germans, thinking it a shame to be left so long out of the picture, and possibly tired of being kept awake, opened with a field battery, an inconsiderate action that effectually damped the proceedings. By one o'clock all was quiet again, and, much to my astonishment, every one returned whole, each man having seen the sniper and had at least a dozen shots at him, every one of which by his own account must have been fatal. Subsequent inquiries revealed the amazing fact that the French also had suffered no casualties. Yet alas! no more, apparently, had the sniper, for the bullets continued to whizz and valuable officers to have hair-breadth escapes until the time came for us to leave the place.

On the next night we were shelled, probably by way of retaliation for the disturbance of the previous night. The enemy seemed to know our approximate position, and " searched and swept " all round us with heavy shell, but never contrived to burst one within twenty yards of the guns. It happened to be my business to walk about the battery, exhorting men to keep under cover. In the middle of it all a party of French soldiers walked nonchalantly through our lines. " Prenez garde," I shouted, " Il y a des obus qui tombe par ici, descendez dans les abris ! " They thanked me and ran into the dug-outs. The next shell burst pretty close, covering everything with fragments. Out dashed my Frenchmen, and in answer to my expostulations, " Nous en voulons un souvenir," they replied, and forthwith began to hunt for the fuse.

Magnificent as are the French infantry, their artillery far surpass them. To those who have any knowledge of artillery work, the French appear as performers of miracles. Their equipment, their incomparable *soixante-quinze*, is a frail-looking cheaply constructed affair, giving the impression of weakness and inefficiency. Their *personnel* seems utterly inadequate, both in men and officers, their methods of ammunition supply are rudimentary. But a French battery will come into action in an inconceivably short time, and will continue in action night and day at a rate of fire that is unbelievable to one who has not heard it. Minor technical details, such as sights, are far in advance of our own, even in the case of some old heavy pieces, whose mirror sight utterly shames by its convenience and simplicity our extraordinary device for the same purpose. And the officers, how keen they were! Scarcely a day passed but some two or three came into the battery and courteously enquired if they might examine *les pièces*. Of course they could, we were only too happy to exhibit them, and then what explanations and comparisons between theirs and ours! " Ce frein-ci n'est pas mal, mais pourquoi les ressorts sont-ils d'une telle longueur? " or " Mon dieu, que cet appareil de portage est compliqué! " Keen men and keen critics, equally eager to show us their weapons and to hear our criticisms upon them. Their colonel included us in his command at such times as we supported the French batteries, which was fairly frequently. A spare figure in a close-fitting jacket, a bullet-shaped head set with a pair of piercing eyes that discovered everything without the assistance of the tongue, he was the ideal of an artillery officer. He had the scientific mind that absorbs every detail and stores it away in a pigeon-hole ready for immediate use. Never once after the first time that I was introduced to him, did he fail, wherever we met, to stop, shake hands and address me by name. In a hurried quarter of an hour I once recited to him all the technical details of the howitzer with which we were armed. Weeks afterwards I heard him repeat faultlessly all the details, with others which he had noticed for himself. If he be a type of the senior artillery officer, happy are our Allies in the possession of such men.

Another incident that occurred to us will show the unvarying promptitude and courtesy with which the French treated us. It happened that close to the battery and in the middle of the French infantry billets was a ruined church tower, of which a certain portion still stood, enough, we discovered, to make it worth our while to build a series of ladders within it, and to use the bell-beam as an emergency observation post. But Monsieur le Poilu thought that this was a capital spot into which to climb, and from thence to wave his képi to his friends and generally to behave in such a manner as to attract the attention of hostile observers, with the not unnatural result that one fine evening the enemy fired a few rounds at it, narrowly missing our senior subaltern, and, which was a matter for far deeper concern, the ration lorry. Complaint being made to the colonel, he, after several complimentary remarks as to our skill in using so unfavourable a place, promised that there should be no repetition of the offence. Ever afterwards an armed guard was posted at the base of the tower, with orders to admit no one but ourselves.

Those French soldiers, what children they were, as their behaviour in the tower showed !

Whenever we were in action, a crowd of them would gather behind the guns to watch the shell in its flight, as is perfectly easy with any low-velocity howitzer. " Venez voir l'obus ! " they would cry, and, as the gun fired, " Le voila, voyez, voyez ! ah, il tombe—— " and a shriek of delight would almost drown one's subsequent orders. What children and what men ! Perfect fighters, eager to rush to the attack, yet patient under the iron discipline of the trenches, easily moved to a wild display of nervous energy, possessing creative imagination, yet stoical under agony to a surpassing degree. And not the men only, but every class—peasants, doctors, priests, each in his own sphere, are imbued with the highest spirit of which man can boast, the spirit of self-sacrifice. I hold no brief for any form of doctrine, being one of those who hold that all religions are nothing but quibbles round a central truth that no sane man denies, but the devotion of the French priest strikes me with the deepest admiration. I have seen a battery heavily shelled and suffer many casualties, so that the detachments were forced to take to their dug-outs. The doctor galloped up on horseback, but the priest on foot, running with his soutane tucked up round his waist, was there first, out in the open administering extreme unction to the mortally wounded, helping others to a place of safety. " Greater love hath no man than this——"

IX

CHANGING POSITION

THE preparation of a battery position is a business that requires much labour and considerable time, if anything more elaborate than mere screening from view is attempted. Deep pits must be dug for the guns, and slopes cut into these pits by which the said guns may be hauled in and out. These pits must be floored with an elaborate platform, their sides must be revetted, that is to say that boards, corrugated iron or some similar substance must be fixed against them to prevent their falling in, and, most difficult feat of all, they must be roofed over with as much earth as such roof beams as can be procured can be made to bear. When the pits are completed, deep caverns must be dug and prepared to serve as refuges for the detachments in case of the battery being shelled. Other shelters must be provided as magazines for ammunition, as a room for the telephone and its operators, as a refuge for the section commanders. Billets must be found for the men and officers, if no billets are available dug-outs must be made. Places must be found for cook-houses, washing-places, work-shops, stores. A battery position prepared for lengthy occupation is a most elaborate work, and one does not light-heartedly desert it for an open plain where everything remains to be done. But sooner or later the dread message comes : " The battery will be pre-pared to move at 6 p.m. to-morrow. An officer will proceed forthwith to such-and-such a place where he will be shown the new position selected." Off goes the officer in the car, he meets some deputy from head-quarters, and the two trudge off together through the ever-present mud. " Here you are," says the deputy cheerfully; " how does this suit you ? Splendid place. Look at that orchard; you could hide the guns under the trees." The battery officer stares glumly at a dozen apple trees, each of which is of a size to flourish contentedly in a fair-sized flower-pot, and makes some dubious reply. " I never knew such difficult fellows to please as you siege battery fellows are in my life ! Well, come and look over here. There's a natural pit, ready dug for you; it'll hold all the battery easily." With this the guide indicates with no little pride a gully, at the bottom of which stagnates rather than flows a greenish liquid with an odour of the most clinging type. " Yes, it might be a bit difficult to get the guns in and out, certainly. What about concealment behind that hedge? " But the hedge proves to be separated from the only road by an impassable morass. At last the orchard is selected as the least impossible under the circumstances, and the officer returns to his battery thoroughly convinced that he has selected the worst possible position on the whole front, and wondering what on earth will be said to him when he exhibits it to the rest of the battery.

Or else the proposed site is in the middle of a village, a place with a reputation for being shelled that is notorious from Ypres to Loos. A fabulous arc of fire is demanded from the battery, and weary hours are spent looking for a more or less concealed spot that will allow of the trajectory clearing houses and trees in all the required directions. At last it is found, the necessary measurements made and found satisfactory, when an officer strolls up. " Good-afternoon. You're

not going to stop here long, are you? Going
to put a battery here! I wouldn't be you
for something, then. I've been about here
for weeks, and they always strafe the school-
house there every day about this time.
Look out, here she comes——" and a " woolly
bear " or a " whizz-bang " or some other
fiendish and aptly named projectile bursts
neatly over the building that one had appro-
priated in one's mind's eye for a mess.
Wearily the search begins again—this might
do, perhaps—but by now the " evening
hate " is in full swing, and a heavy shell
settles with a self-satisfied " crrrump ! " in
the middle of one's oasis, digging one's
gun-pits before one's eyes, as it were.

On one occasion the position chosen for
us was the really beautiful garden of a
medium-sized château. The front was a
well-planned mass of shrubbery, intersected
with paths and flower-beds, the back a
walled vegetable garden, most scrupulously
maintained, planted with every sort of
vegetable and fruit and provided with a
good range of glass. The owner of the
place lived in the château, and his gardener
worked on the premises. The dismay of
these good people when they were told that
the place was to be turned into a battery

and the men billeted in the château can
better be imagined than described. The
owner was a philosopher, and took matters
calmly. " Enfin, c'est la guerre, que voulez-
vous ? " he said sadly as we expressed our
horror at the necessity of ruining this little
paradise. The gardener was no philosopher,
and when I look back upon the mutilated
shrubberies, the trodden-down grass plots,
the hotbeds with their boarding torn up
for revetment, the old wall breached in
many places for easy access, the broken
panes in the greenhouses and, worst of all,
four yawning chasms where once the aspara-
gus, the strawberries and the artichokes
dwelt together in amity, I do not wonder
at the hostile spirit he displayed. I can
see him now dancing round the sergeant-
major, an imperturbable person of few words
in his own tongue, and of none in French,
whom he found cutting a few cabbages for
the sergeants' dinner. " Sacré nom d'un
cochon, regardez-là le voleur qui arrache
mes petits choux ! Ah, les anglais sont
incroyables ! " " No compree," says the
sergeant-major, and goes on with his garner-
ing. The gardener got something of his
own back that night, however, for the garden
had a very complete system of hydrants all

over it, which same hydrants our friend stealthily visited with the turn-key, which he then disposed of and departed. It was pitch dark and we were all busy working, so that it was some time before we noticed the gathering floods, and the whole place was inches deep in mud and water by the time that we had discovered how to turn it off again. We never brought the crime home to the criminal, but a certain hidden gleam of triumph in that gardener's wholly disapproving eye has always convinced me of his guilt.

We had much to contend with in occupying that position. Several times we were held up in our work, first by somebody who said the situation was too exposed and that it was sheer suicide to occupy a house that was conspicuous for miles round; then by the urgent representations of a French officer who commanded a battery near by, and who declared that we should draw down fire upon the devoted heads of his people; and finally by a conference who debated for some time whether we were really required in that sector at all. However, we got all these matters satisfactorily settled at last, and set to work in earnest. And digging pits by night in the light of

L

a few hurricane lamps is work indeed, especially if it rains persistently, as it almost invariably does. Unskilful wielders of the pick are apt to drive their lethal weapons into everything but the ground they mean to excavate, their favourite targets being such parts of their neighbours as get in their way. This leads to acrimonious wrangling and consequent delay. Better this, however, than the adventure of one lusty champion, who with a mighty effort drove his pick clean through the cast-iron main that supplied the delinquent hydrants, whereby he converted, in an incredibly short space of time, that half-completed pit into a sea of mud and water some four feet deep. To any one who expresses a fondness for bathing I recommend the plugging of a four-inch main, with a good pressure behind it, lying at the bottom of four feet of a cream-like mixture of chalk, clay and water at three o'clock on an autumn morning.

Geology, we are told, is the science that deals with the constitutents of the earth. A new chapter should be written to the text-books, a new branch of the science has been rendered necessary by the war, the study of the properties of mud. Mud is now elevated to the dignity of a fifth element, but surpasses the other four by its perpetual presence, equalled only by that of the ether which pervades everything we know. Mud shares its motto with the Royal Regiment of Artillery, one lives in it, sleeps in it, and not infrequently eats it—indeed, competent experts with carefully trained palates are said to be able to tell from the flavour of the bacon at breakfast the exact part of the line in which it has been rolled before issue. Surely in all the ancient mythologies some student may find for mud some presiding deity that we may suitably propitiate?

Nor were such more or less natural phenomena our only hindrances. No sooner were the pits completed, than somebody more perspicacious than his fellows discovered that we had been ordered to lay them out in the wrong direction, and they had to be cut out still further to allow the platforms to be slewed round through the required angle. This order reached us one evening just as we were promising ourselves a night in bed after our strenuous labours, and the despair of all ranks spread like a mephitic vapour over the countryside in a mist of strange profanity. The men, however, whose spirits are proof against continued despondency under the most depressing circumstances, set to work with a will, and the tedious digging was finished at last. Then came the far more interesting business of revetting and roofing. Now, obviously revetting and roofing require planks, beams, iron sheets, and material of that nature, and equally obviously the department that professes to provide stores of this description, and whose imagination rarely soars above the level of sandbags, is utterly unable to supply such things. The only course left is to find them for oneself, and fortunately a row of houses whose inhabitants had been evicted stood on this occasion near at hand, and these we gutted. Doors, shutters, floor-boards, rafters, everything but the bricks themselves, we contrived to utilize, until we had everything we could desire except girders for our roofs, which were to be of earth. Now a fifteen-foot span of earth two feet in thickness requires a good deal of supporting, and after several experiments with rafters, experiments that sometimes had unpleasant results for those who conducted them, we decided that something stronger was required. Here, again, almost in the manner of the Swiss Family Robinson, we found what we re-

quired at our very door, but not before one
adventurous spirit had invited an early
death (from which may he long be spared !)
by driving a particularly noisy lorry into
a coal mine overlooking the German lines
in search of pit-props. Our discovery was
due to an eagle eye that discovered a notice-
board bearing the words " Défense de circuler
sur la voie," whose owner, realizing that
there could be no temptation to circulate
on the line if there was no line upon which
to circulate, investigated further and found
a grass-grown colliery siding. Here were
our long-sought girders, and with their
discovery our troubles were practically over.
Certainly the guns had yet to be lowered
into the pits, and hauling heavy guns over
soft garden mould on a dark night is an
undertaking to try the most angelic patience,
but on this occasion, for the first and last
time, the Mud-god smiled upon us, and that
midnight we knew the true happiness that
comes of the successful completion of
strenuous labour.

Here we remained for some weeks, until
again disturbed by the order to change
position. Again everything has to be done
by night, the guns hauled out of the pits,
the thousand and one small stores necessary

to the interior economy of the battery
packed each in its proper place, the heavy
platforms raised and loaded into the lorries.
The ease with which any particular article
can be mislaid under those circumstances
is incredible. Relative weight or importance
seems to have no bearing on the matter at
all, one is just as likely, upon arriving at
dawn in some unknown land, to discover
that one has left behind a spare wheel or
a handcart or even a battery quartermaster-
sergeant, as one is to find a small screw-
driver missing. After a while the whole
business becomes a nightmare in which
one is condemned eternally to spend one's
time counting handspikes and lorries and
men, and to make the total utterly different
every time. And then the line of march!
A procession of heavy lorries, some drawing
the guns, the rest laden with men, stores
and ammunition, looking for all the world
like some huge travelling circus, sets off
upon a dark foggy night, carrying of course
no lights, over roads already laden to their
utmost capacity with troops and supply
columns, and plentifully besprinkled with
shell holes. At the head of the procession
rides a group of officers in a car, one of whom
has possibly been over the road once by

daylight, and about the length of the convoy are scattered here and there men wrestling with recalcitrant motor-bicycles, which they vainly try to restrict to the speed of the column, perhaps four or five miles an hour. Much can happen under these circumstances. Perhaps the rearmost lorry has to stop for adjustment, and by the time the word has passed along the line the car at the head is far away, and the column strung out over a mile or so of road. Or the foremost lorry commences to boil frantically and slows down, whereupon the remainder tread upon one another's heels, until it stops altogether, when the column forms a compact mass that nothing can attempt to pass. Or the geographical instinct of the leader of the expedition fails at a cross-roads, and recourse has to be had to the sentry who stands there. One of two things then happens. Either the man does not know the way and says so, or he does not know the way and with the utmost positiveness declares the route to be by the first road that strikes his fancy. Those to whom the former of these certainties happens are by far the most fortunate, for the attempt to turn a column of lorries on a narrow road, especially if it consists, as it usually does,

of a central strip of pavé bordered by
fathomless mud, is certain to be fraught
with disaster. A fully-loaded ammunition
lorry stuck in a ditch is a most heartbreaking
sight, particularly (if the bull may be for-
given) if the night is so dark that one cannot
see it. It must be unloaded, dragged out
by the help of another lorry, which sometimes
slides into the ditch itself in the process,
and then loaded up again, usually to the
accompaniment of uncomplimentary observations from the traffic that it is holding up.

Certainly the accidents that may happen
to mechanical transport are many and
various, but there are some to which it
is not liable. One of the first messages that
we received upon our arrival in a certain
new position ran as follows, " Report at
once all cases of glanders occurring amongst
your transport." One has trouble enough
without infectious disease to contend with.
A motor lorry is a capital thing on a road,
even if that road is in a very bad state,
but, once take it on to soft or slippery
ground, and its imperfections become mani-
fest. First of all its wheels start to slip,
and chains are fixed round the felloes to
give them a grip. This answers for a while,
but suddenly the wheels begin to revolve

at a terrific speed, and the chains fly hurtling through the air to the obvious disadvantage of any one who gets in their way. A few men with lamps are sent to look for these, whilst the rest endeavour to give the lorry a start by pushing behind. Start she does, with a sudden leap, and, before she can be stopped, finds the softest part of the whole field and sinks gently but firmly into it until supported on her axles. By this time the search party, having taken all the lanterns with them, is far away, and you feel the lorry sinking without a possibility of doing anything by the light of the one match that the battery possesses. The only thing left to do is to dig her out, support her wheels on planks, and haul her on to the road again with ropes.

But the march ends at last, usually at about two o'clock in the morning, and one arrives tired, cold and very sleepy, in the unknown land. This village is the place we were told to stop at, and the men's billets are said to be somewhere over there. Glad of a walk, I set out to find them, and find in succession a row of tents knee-deep in mud, apparently completely surrounded by barbed wire entanglements, a barn without a roof, and a shed tenanted by two

inquisitive and particularly skittish cows.
I return to the lorries and find the men
drawn up at the side of the road. Having
explained the situation, I call for volunteers
to spend the night with the cows. The
country-bred members of the battery fall out
and are marched off to deal with the fierce
beasts as best they can. The remainder
are carefully shepherded into the roofless
barn and the bottomless tents. Judging
by the language that arises, this latter
party are foiled in their first attack by the
wire. But the gunner is an adaptable
person, and all contrive to settle themselves
as comfortably as possible in a wonderfully
short time, leaving me free to find the
officer's billet, which turns out to be the
drawing-room of a small miller's house.
The only corner left is under the grand
piano, and there I lay out my valise and
am soon fast asleep. Let the troubles of
the morning care for themselves!

X

TELEPHONES

THE Field Telephone system, that is to say a series of portable telephone instruments connected by a wire laid as required, forms the nervous system of every battery, without which it is useless, or at all events so heavily handicapped that it might as well be out of action. The observing officer depends upon it to transmit his orders to the guns, the group or brigade commander transmits his instructions to his battery commander by its means, and in the battery itself it is used for intercommunication between the control station, the section commanders, billets and other points. All these various lines must be laid as soon as the battery comes into position, and once laid they must be kept under constant supervision. The test of the efficiency of any battery is first the accuracy of its shooting, and second its ability to bring fire to bear upon any point in its area immediately it is ordered to do so. And experience shows that failure in either of these respects can be traced in nearly every case to some factor connected with the telephone system, an instrument or line being out of order at the critical moment, or an inattentive or careless telephonist. It is easy to realize, therefore, the importance of the part played by this instrument in modern artillery practice, and some account of its habits may not be out of place as throwing light upon a particularly interesting phase of life in the zone of war.

The line between the battery and the observation post is the most important of the whole system, for, without it, properly directed fire is impossible. It is also, from the fact that the observation post is usually close to the front line, the most exposed, and therefore most liable to accident. To lay a wire between two given points may seem to be the simplest thing in the world, as indeed it is, but so to lay that wire that it will not constantly be cut is a fine art. There are two ways of laying it, overhead amongst trees and other supports, or underground, digging a narrow trench in which

to bury it.   The first method is the quickest,
and if a line is required for use immediately,
the best plan is to lay it overhead, and bury
it subsequently if required.   But many perils
lie in wait for an overhead line.   Lay it by
any route you will, some wandering shrapnel
will burst near by, and one of the bullets,
singling out the wire as though it were its
especial target, will cut it neatly through,
for preference at its most inaccessible point.
But the enemy is by no means its greatest
danger.   There are roads to cross, along
which come heavy lorries laden high with
stores of all kinds.   Put the line up as high
as you think absolutely safe, and sooner or
later an extra tall load brings it down.   Or
natural support, such as trees or houses, fails,
and at considerable pains you plant a row
of light posts.   The next party of wire
layers that comes along, finding these convenient to their purpose, lay their own line
on them in addition.   So the process continues, until the light posts, that you designed
to carry one wire only, collapse under the
strain, and down comes the whole tangle.
Worst of all are the unpardonable crimes of
some miscreants, who, running short of wire,
cut off as much from your line as they

require, leaving the cable with a yawning gulf in the middle, or, as a variation, tap their own instruments on to the wire, when the unfortunate observation officer is left to play a maddening game of cross questions and crooked answers with some strange unknown battery. If, on the other hand, the wire is laid underground, a high-explosive shell is sure to find it and make a neat crater in the middle of it, or else the infantry dig a communication trench across it, or its insulation breaks down late one evening and the ensuing night is spent digging it up and looking for the fault.

The best method of ensuring unbroken communication between two points is, of course, to lay more than one line, but wire is usually scarce, and this course is not always possible. Even if this is done, there must be places where the lines run close together, and these are just the places where the shells are sure to drop. During the Four Days' bombardment we had three lines between the battery and our observation post, and on two separate occasions all three were cut at the same time by shell-fire. The quiet deeds of heroism performed by artillery telephonists that are never heard of would fill a volume by themselves. There is very little of the excitement and emulation that makes many a man in the midst of his comrades the hero of a glorious moment, none of the intoxication of battle that banishes all thought of personal safety, in the experiences of a man who goes out to repair a wire under fire. He has plenty of time to think of the dangers he is running, to anticipate the fall of every shell without being able to get out of its way, to wonder what it feels like to lie in agony on the ground, torn by a splinter. Slowly and alone he must follow the track of the wire until he finds the break, and having found it he must set to work to repair it where it lies, a proceeding that may often take a very considerable time. And it is more than probable that nobody but himself and his chum ever knows anything about it. Yet there is never the least hesitation on his part to go out; on one of the occasions mentioned when our lines were cut, the linesman picked up his tools and started along the line as a matter of course, although the determined nature of the hostile shelling was plainly visible, and some of the projectiles were charged with gas. He finished his job and came back to us full of his adventures, which seemed to afford him immense amusement; indeed, I think he was one of those who have learnt that the surest safeguard against fear is a sense of humour, and that danger, if treated as a huge joke, ceases to have any terrors.

And quite apart from actual danger, the linesman's life is a troubled one. As one never knows when the lines may not be required in a hurry, telephonists and linesmen relieve one another day and night. Every few minutes the stations ring one another up, and if no reply can be obtained, the linesman at the calling station starts along the line to find the fault and repair it. It may be that the wire has been cut by shell-fire, or by accidents inherent to its nature, or by the sinful practices of others. Or again, it may sometimes happen that the linesman proceeds on his way, testing as he goes, and finding all correct, until at last he reaches the other station, to discover that the operator there has for some reason disconnected his instrument and forgotten to connect it up again, in which case a lurid and fiery scene takes place, consisting of picturesque recrimination on the part of the

outraged linesman, and no less picturesque
expostulation on the part of the telephonist,
to the effect that it was somebody else's fault.
The acrimony displayed varies directly as the
temper of the disputants and the distance
between the two stations.

It is extremely difficult to train men to
use a telephone intelligently, far more so
than to teach them the mere technical
details of its construction. Because the
thing appears to talk, very few people can
resist the impulse to treat it as a sentient
being, intentionally perverse for the express
purpose of annoyance. Ring up your best
friend in peace time on a slightly defective
instrument and observe how he or she
treats the irresponsive toy. If a man, he
will grow purple in the face and swear, he
may even end by casting the offending thing
on the ground and trampling upon it in his
fury, if a woman she will grow tearful and
excessively petulant, and will certainly pour
the vials of her wrath upon you, as being
the proximate cause of the trouble. Even
so in time of war it is the tendency of the
trained telephonist to use harsh words and
report the instrument out of action instead
of sitting down quietly and finding the cause

M

of the trouble, which he knows perfectly well how to do. Even the best of them can never refrain from shaking the receiver viciously by way of punctuating every sentence, they having been rashly taught by their instructor that a gentle tap on the speaking end of the concern is often useful if speech is faint. And even when this tendency to violence, apparently a component of human nature, is eradicated, there comes the surpassing difficulty of inducing men to speak clearly and distinctly. Of course men of clear speech must be selected in the first place, the uncouth dialects of certain parts of the United Kingdom being not susceptible to the gentlest treatment. For instance, two telephonists, one hailing from Glasgow and the other from the wilds of Glamorgan, will utterly fail to make themselves intelligible to one another. On one occasion a certain dour Scotch subaltern was told to select from his section the six men with the clearest voice and purest accent for training as telephonists. He did so, and they were duly tested—they all spoke a strange tongue which proved upon investigation to be the broadest Scotch! To this day that subaltern cannot understand why they were rejected and he himself loaded with opprobrious epithets.

At one time we were in a position where the French wireless bulletin was transmitted to us in the original over the telephone. The state in which it reached us frequently defied translation, as may well be imagined. I once overheard a reference to the Hartmansweilerkopf coming through. " Are man's wily coughs *wot ?* 'Ere, is this a patent medicine advertisement, or wot ? Hullo, hullo ! Goin' to spell it, are yer ? Yes, haitch for 'energy, eye for what ? Oh, eye for hass, r for rum, toc, emma, eye for hass, n for Nellie, esses, w for water —'ere, hullo, hullo ! What the 'ell are yer gettin' at ? " After that they took to sending it by Morse code on the buzzer, and things went along more smoothly, but even then it was a mutilated word that eventually reached me. From which it may be inferred that telephone messages do not always find the recipient in the same form in which they started, especially if they have to be repeated more than once during transmission. The story of the Loos refugees is a case in point.

In addition to the complexities introduced by human failings, the telephone in the field suffers from aberrations of technical origin. Owing to the fact that the earth is used as the path for the return current in nearly every case, an instrument, if sufficiently sensitive, will pick up scraps of conversation between two stations speaking to one another, if the line joining them crosses or approaches to the line joining its own stations. In the case of the territory occupied by a modern army, wherein the chief means of communication is the telephone, extraordinary results are sometimes obtained. I have frequently slept with the receiver of a telephone close to my ear, and in the silence of the night have heard it whispering all sorts of fragmentary messages—" Hullo, hullo, brigade, are you brigade ? brigade !— yes, and the old man was awfully fed up about it—brigade, brigade, hullo, can you hear me ?—lengthen a hundred, fuse forty-two and a half ! " and so on, *pianissimo*, throughout the night. Both sides have frequently obtained valuable information by putting specially sensitive telephones as near as possible to the opposing trenches and listening to the messages they picked up. It is believed that the apparently miraculous

knowledge that the Germans at some parts
of the line possessed as to the regiments
opposed to them—they would often call out,
" Hullo, Rutlandshires, are you in yet ? "
when a totally fresh battalion took over a
section of trenches—was obtained by this
method. Nor is this earth leakage the only
way in which conversations are overheard.
If two or more lines run together for any
considerable distance, as in practice they
often must, owing to an electrical phenomenon known as induction, a conversation
taking place along one line is audible in the
receivers attached to the remainder. Further,
it frequently happens that owing to a shell
burst or to carelessness on the part of some
line layer, a pole or other support to which
a large number of lines are fixed is brought
down, and in its fall all the lines are broken.
It may often be very difficult to discover,
amongst all the ends, which belongs to which,
and an inexperienced man, actuated by a
sincere and laudable desire to put matters
right, is very apt to connect them up by the
light of nature. The consequent confusion
that arises must provoke to demoniac
laughter the denizens of hell. One observation officer finds himself in direct and clear

communication with the officer in charge of supplies and transport, another with an advanced dressing station. Infantry headquarters hold long and heated converse with the wagon line of a field battery, the G. O. C. Divisional Artillery threatens to place the quartermaster of a territorial battalion under arrest because he steadfastly refuses to open fire immediately on target Z. And a considerable time elapses before all these various people are again connected to the proper quarter.

The very form of the telephonic message lends itself to misinterpretation and misunderstanding. There is a story of an officer named Close, who as forward observation officer for his battery laid out a line to an observation post of his own choosing, and whose linesmen by some accident contrived to get their wire touching one belonging to a different system. His major, wishing to speak to him, called him up, and hearing a " Hullo ! " in reply, began " Are you Close ? " To his astonishment and delight a strange voice replied, " No, you dam ! fool, I'm five thousand yards away ! " This same crossing of wires is another common cause of mixed conversations, they chafe one another until the insulation is worn away and a good connection established, when the two sets of instruments respond to one another's calls. This very trouble was the cause of my once being awakened from sleep by the urgent summons of the buzzer. I jumped for the instrument—" Yes, hullo? " And then distinctly came the amazing query " Are you St. Paul? " I think the terms of my reply, in which I convinced my unknown questioner of my utter inability to follow that gentleman's advice about suffering fools gladly, satisfied him that I was not. I found out afterwards that a neighbouring battery had two observing stations, which they had christened Westminster Abbey and St. Paul's respectively. An error in transcription, whereby the singular became substituted for the plural, was probably the cause of my receiving a written message, warning me that certain experiments were to be tried that evening, and beginning in the emphatic terms, " At 6 p.m. some rocket will be fired."

Of the whole complex system of lines, that between headquarters (which in our case is the group commander, batteries being usually organized in groups under a senior

officer) and the battery commander is by
far the most fertile in trouble. It is not so
much the line itself that is to blame, as a sort
of nervous feeling that it connects one with
one's superior officer, a feeling that in a
wholly indefinable way pervades everybody
who comes in contact with it. If, as frequently occurs, wire is saved by leading the
various battery lines to an exchange, whence
a single line runs back to headquarters, the
possibility of complication is enormously
increased. The process of getting a message
through is then a nerve-racking one. I
was once assisting the battery commander
in the observation post, observing a series
that was of some considerable importance
—it was during the fighting round Hill 70.
In the middle of the transmission of orders
to the battery, an interruption comes
through from them. "Headquarters want
to speak to the major, sir!" "Never mind
headquarters, you take my message."
Three minutes elapse, during which we get
off a few more rounds. Then the battery
calls through again, "Headquarters say
it's urgent, sir!" "All right, stop firing,
switch them through." A long pause,
during which the receiver echoes, "Hullo,

hullo, exchange! Hullo, can you hear me?
I want headquarters. Hullo! Speaking to
another battery are they? Hullo, is that
headquarters? I'm 320th Siege—here you
are, sir." Then a still small voice, "Am I
speaking to the major?" "I'm taking the
message for him; go on." "Message from
G. O. C. Corps Artillery, begins. Please
report by noon on 30th instant number of
Army Forms XY 9999 in your possession,
ends. For your information and compliance
please." Fortunately Job was a hasty and
impetuous individual compared with the
major, or his remarks on having wasted a
quarter of an hour of rapidly failing light
to receive such a message might have been
unthinkable.

I remember also on that same line another
regrettable incident. We had to render a
certain report daily at a certain hour, and
one day the headquarters line suddenly
went out of action a few minutes before this
time. The report was sent off by hand, and
the linesman started on his weary journey
of investigation. He reached the exchange
eventually, testing every inch as he went,
and found at last that the wire was not
properly connected to the switchboard in

the exchange itself.   Now all this took some considerable time, and it was not till some hours later that a scared-looking telephonist found me in the battery and asked me to come to the telephone, as there was somebody at headquarters " a-carrying-on something hawful." So I went and found an infuriated and temporary officer demanding that I should immediately put all the telephonists under arrest and myself into the bargain—I think all the officers were included. Explaining that there might be difficulties in working the battery if those instructions were faithfully carried out, I asked what our crime had been. It then appeared that our messenger had arrived five minutes late with the report. I explained how this happened, pointed out that his own people at the exchange were to blame, and offered, should he consider mere arrest to be too trivial a punishment for men who had delayed the receipt of a purely routine report—it consisted of one word, nil !—by five minutes, to send him down a firing party at once. We never had any further trouble on that particular score.

As an alternative to the telephone, it is sometimes possible to arrange relays of signallers with visual means of communication, such as lamps or signalling discs, a method very much more freely employed by the Germans than by ourselves.

We established a chain of this nature along a line of a total length of about a mile and a half, as an emergency measure in case the wires should be cut, and on the occasion of a very critical moment when this disaster actually occurred, we found the system to work admirably. For general use, however, it is too slow and requires too many trained signallers. The telephone, in spite of all its peculiar idiosyncrasies, is the only method in practice it is possible to employ.

It will be gathered from the above that a battery requires a very large number of instruments and apparatus of all descriptions, and the strain upon the manufacturers to supply them fast enough to equip new formations was at one time very great. In our own case, some of these stores only reached us on the quay of the port of embarkation an hour before the transport sailed. We had been toiling since early morning on one of the hottest days of the year, with no possible opportunity for refreshment. A car dashed up and unloaded a box of instruments, which we proceeded to unpack for the purpose of checking. The first thing to be produced was a large aneroid barometer, of which the hand pointed significantly to the words " Very dry." A sagacious instrument was that.

XI

BEHIND THE LINE

" Upon the Western Front there is nothing to report." So runs the official news from day to day; it is a period of comparative quiet in which neither army finds it expedient to make a move, but each lies watching and waiting for the next sign of activity on the part of the other. It is not inactivity, the perpetual crack of rifles and the occasional bursts of artillery fire that rise suddenly by day and night are the surest guarantees of that, but merely the temporary abandonment of offensive tactics on either side. Modern trench warfare has strengthened the defence at the expense of the offence to so great an extent that such periods must be the natural state of things. There is no such thing as a flank attack, for the flanks of the opposing forces rest upon positions that cannot be turned, in one case the sea, in the other a neutral country. Many years ago, long before

such an extended double defensive was contemplated, an extremely clever parody upon
the art of war as laid down in the textbooks
was produced, in which the author sets forth
three possible means of collision, first when
two armies meet, both of which are in motion,
second when two armies meet, one of which
is in motion and the other is stationary, and
third when two armies meet both of which
are stationary. The latter situation, ridicu-
lous as it appears and as the author intended it to appear, is the best definition of
the state of things which actually occurs daily
along all the gigantic fronts. " Nothing
doing," says the gunner; " we fired a few
rounds yesterday at a place where somebody
said the Bosches had a battery, but that's
all." " Haven't seen a bullet or a shell for
days," says the infantryman. " Believe
there's nobody but the caretaker and his
wife opposite." In the battery we have
meals at regular hours, we discuss the war
instead of our own infinitesimal contribution
to it, the more enterprising amongst us hint
at the glorious possibilities of having a hot
bath. Life, in short, begins to slip into a
groove of routine.

Yet we are in a state of constant readiness,
and the appearance of inactivity is wholly

misleading. Eyes are perpetually on the watch in the observation station, a telephonist sits with the head receiver of the instrument fixed on his head, the detachments on duty sit in the gun-pits or in the dug-outs close at hand, busy upon some work, improving the head cover, polishing the fittings of the gun, or else writing letters to their friends that tell strange tales of battle, murder and sudden death. In the control room by the telephone dug-out sits an officer, studying the map, recording the results of a previous day's fire, or entering particulars of targets and ranges in his note-book. Perhaps the wind is blowing towards the firing line, carrying away from the battery all sounds of war, so that nothing can be heard but the strains of an amateur band (of mouthorgans, concertinas and a triangle) from one of the gun-pits, and the monotonous call of the crier in that strange game of " House " that pervades the British Army—" nineteen, forty-one, number three, sixty-four," and a sudden excited voice " 'ouse ! "

But suddenly the buzzer in the telephone room wakes into life. Dash dot dot dash, dash dot dot, dash dash dot—X D G, it calls imperiously. That is our call, and the telephonist throws away the novel he was reading and seizes pencil and paper. "320th Siege! Yes, go on, yes—fire six rounds at once on Puits thirty-seven. R.D." The message reaches the officer in the control room, who dashes out of the door with a megaphone through which he roars one word, "Action!" Instantly the detachments vanish into the pits, from which a sound of urgent preparation rises, the band stops abruptly upon an excruciating chord, the players of "House" scatter to their respective stations. Then comes the regular sequence of orders, and in something less than a minute from the receipt of the message the first gun roars into pulsing life again.

Sudden calls such as these are only incidents that disturb the quiet of the daily life of the battery, which pursues the even tenor of its way as soon as the number of rounds ordered has been fired. And even when the word "Action!" sounds, it only affects the officers and men actually on duty. The remainder are free to follow their own vocations until it is their turn to be ready to answer the summons. There is usually plenty of work for officers off duty to do, in the battery itself, but still several opportunities occur for exploration of the neighbouring country, of which the most

interesting form is reconnaissance of the
ground from the front line trenches in one's
own neighbourhood.   I have had many
most interesting excursions to places from
whence a different view of the country could
be obtained from that presented from our
own observation stations, and a different
angle of view often clears up many doubtful
points.   It is a most difficult matter to
recognize every feature on the ground by
the aid of a map from one point alone, but
if angles can be taken to a doubtful object
from two or more points, its position can
be fixed and identified upon the map with
comparative ease.   And the interest of an
expedition taken with this primary object
in view lies in the unexpected discoveries
that one often makes, of objects and incidents
that would otherwise be unknown to one.
In the southern sector the village of Loos
was a favourite object for a walk.   The
enemy kept the place continuously under
fire after his repulse from it, to such an
extent that the establishment there of a
permanent observation station was sternly
discouraged by the higher artillery command.
It is useless to risk the lives of telephonists
and linesmen in a place that is under fire
night and day, and where, even if one's

N

observation station is spared, one's lines are certain to be repeatedly cut, unless the objects to be gained by so doing are of counterbalancing importance. We were lucky enough to possess other and safer observation posts, so that we only used the village in cases of necessity. And we were by no means sorry, for, to use the deathless expression of Monsieur le Commandant, the place was " not sanitary," not only from the effects of the enemy's fire, but from the fact that for many weeks after the operations of September 25 the streets were still encumbered with dead horses and other odoriferous objects. Even as late as the third week in October the dead lay thickly strewn outside the cover afforded by the houses, and on a still day the stench in the particular building that we used as a watch-tower was utterly insupportable unless one smoked without intermission. It used to be said that it was possible to find one's way about the place in the dark purely by the use of one's nose alone.

During another of these journeys of exploration, one of our officers was in the front line trenches, which had recently been slightly pushed forward, engaged in marking them in on his map. The trenches were newly

dug and not yet finished, and the enemy,
knowing this, kept up a slow but fairly
steady rain of shrapnel upon them.   As my
friend was making his way along the trench,
he saw a brigadier and his entourage advancing in the opposite direction towards him.
Having an instinctive mistrust of " brass-
hats " and of the inane questions that they
are so fond of asking, he stopped where he
was, hoping that they would pass by without noticing him.   But the fates were
against him.   When not more than twenty
yards separated him from the splendid
company, a shell burst fairly in the trench
not a couple of yards from the brigadier
himself, damaging neither him nor his staff,
but unfortunately killing one of the defenders.   Almost at the same moment one
of the lynx-eyed suite discovered my friend's
presence and also the fact that he was an
artillery officer.   " Just the man we want !
Order your battery to open fire at once on
the gun that fired that shot."   To the
average staff officer politeness is a sign of
weakness, nothing but a peremptory order
is possible from one of such high mental
attainments.   My friend explained with some
asperity that he was not in communication
with his battery, being merely on a recon-

naissance for the purpose of discovering
information that the Staff had neglected to
render, information that was of vital importance, namely the position of our own
trenches. But that if he would be good
enough to inform him of the exact position
of the offending battery, he would walk
back and open fire upon it. Then all the
members of the entourage—the brigadier
himself maintained an amused silence
throughout—pointed in different directions,
each swearing that they had seen the flash
of the gun in the place he indicated, some of
them displaying a happy ignorance by select-
ing places well within our own lines. My
friend was to take a compass bearing of the
direction, he was to stand where the shell
fell and wait for the next flash (not a bad
idea that), they themselves would get into
touch with the artillery group through
their own telephone system. Finally they
drifted on, still, like the heathen, furiously
raging together. My friend forgot all about
them in the course of investigating more
important matters, until he arrived that
evening at the office of his group commander to report upon his observations.
He was greeted with the words, " Hullo,
what have you been up to ? " " Nothing

particularly heinous, I hope, sir." "What did you tell that parcel of lunatics to ring me up and request me to open fire on nothing for?" "I didn't, sir," and then the whole story came out, much to the amusement of the group commander. Nor did this close the incident by any means. Somebody having decided that the battery that had the presumption to fire upon a brigadier and his staff was probably situated in a certain wood, on the morrow of the affair at a given hour every battery within range was ordered to fire a certain number of rounds into the said wood. The result must have saved the enemy the trouble of cutting firewood for the rest of the winter.

When not engaged upon reconnaissance, there is always plenty of interest in the battery itself, of which a large proportion is provided by the aeroplanes of both sides. However carefully the battery itself may be concealed, this precaution is useless unless the *personnel* keep out of sight when hostile aeroplanes are about. Men do not stand about in groups for the fun of the thing, there must be some military reason for it, or, everything else failing, it is probably an indication of a billeting area. At all events, it is worth trying a few rounds at for luck, or so the German gunners seem to think. An aeroplane sentry armed with a pair of glasses and a whistle is consequently perpetually on duty, and the blast of his whistle is the signal for everybody to get under cover at once. It becomes very trying to get into the habit of leaving whatever one is doing and take shelter under the nearest tree several times in the hour, and if, for instance, one is digging gun-pits against time the annoyance is maddening. But neglect of this precaution is sure sooner or later to have fatal results. On one occasion the men of a French battery in a field close to us treated a reconnoitring Taube with the most profound contempt, they were building shelters and refused to stop work for so trivial a cause. We, more cautious, bolted for cover and stayed there while the hostile aeroplane, having evidently noticed something, circled round once or twice, and then, when directly over the French battery, dropped some tinsel substance that sparkled in the sun, as an indication to the artillery of the whereabouts of its quarry. And sure enough next morning we were treated to a really magnificent display of accurate shooting. A German battery opened fire without warning, leaving just sufficient time for the men to rush into their dug-outs before the second shell burst fairly in the centre of the battery. They fired very few rounds, but a lucky shell burst in a hay-stack behind which were hidden the battery ammunition wagons, setting it on fire. The result was very interesting. For an hour or more the air was thick with cartridge cases and fragments of shell, as the ammunition in the wagons slowly caught fire. There was no sudden explosion, and beyond the utter destruction of the wagons very little damage was done, but regarded as a pyrotechnic display the scene in that field was very hard to beat.

But the reconnoitring aeroplane is by no means allowed to have things all its own way. Anti-aircraft guns fill the space about it with bursting shrapnel, other aeroplanes rise to attack it, machine guns spit bullets at it. If no damage is done, the unfortunate observer is kept far too busy to worry about what is going on down below him. On one occasion we were conducting a series by the help of aerial observation. It was a beautifully clear day, and to our astonishment our first three rounds were signalled " Not observed." Then came a message, " Observation impossible, am coming home," and in about a minute we saw our aeroplane " coming home " at top speed, closely pursued by three hostile machines. Sometimes one is fortunate enough to witness an air duel, which is one of the most magnificent sights imaginable. The anti-aircraft guns are silent, the risk of hitting their friends is too great, and high up above the ground the machines wheel and turn and dive at angles that seem incredible to the watchers below. Very faintly comes the roar of the engines and the staccato rattle of machine guns and automatic pistols. At last one of the machines, finding itself overpowered, dives suddenly, and then, straightening its course, makes a long vol plané to the safety of its own lines, followed by its antagonists till the anti-aircraft fire becomes too hot for them. Or there is a sudden silence, a curious fluttering as of a winged bird, and, quite slowly as it seems, a torn mass of metal and canvas dives headlong to earth. Or perhaps one morning a dull drone attracts one's attention, and, looking up, one sees against the deep blue of the sky an aerial squadron, their wings almost pure white in the sun, a flight of sinister wild geese, carrying bombs to the destruction of some important railway centre. Flanders is much to be recommended as a suitable spot in which to undergo the cure of ennui.

The men off duty seem also to find plenty of occupation. For one thing there is always something to grumble at—either it rains, and the billets leak water through their broken-down roofs, or the mail does not arrive one day, or something of the kind happens—for the gunner is an inveterate " grouser " at trifles, although such incidents as being shelled only seem to amuse him. And then he can go to the nearest spot in which the inhabitants have still been allowed to remain, where he finds every cottage converted into an *estaminet*. There he may sit with a group of his friends drinking that strange beer that is about as intoxicating as tea and not quite so harmful, and he can grumble at that. Gunner Wolverhampton, the sheen upon whose nose indicates that he is probably something of a connoisseur in the matter of beer, says that it tastes like the water that mother washes the onions in, and I daresay it does. Here, sitting in these cottage parlours, you find him holding long conversations with their owners and perhaps a handful of French soldiers, in the curious language that is rapidly growing up. If there should be a girl in the place (her

age or looks are quite immaterial) he cannot refrain from chaff. "You compree
promnade?" he says. "Si, si," she replies.
"Well, you come promnade with moi down
the route, savvy?" She shakes her head.
"You no bon," he says gravely. "Mais
oui, moi j'suis bonne, mais vous méchant."
"No bon, my dear, but portez two beers,
twoppence, compree?" The way the two
nations understand one another is amazing.
"The old girl at the farm was telling me last
night all about the time when the Bosches
was here," said Gunner Wolverhampton to
me one day. "How on earth did you
manage to understand her?" I asked. "Oh,
we got along famous," he replied, and very
soon showed me that she had made him
understand her remarks thoroughly. On
one occasion, finding a party of French
linesmen stranded for a length of wire, one
of our telephonists gave them a piece, and
ever afterwards the two batteries were on
terms of the greatest intimacy. The men
used to go and sit in one another's billets,
frequently, after the manner of their kind,
exchanging headgear as they did so, with
the most curious effects, as when a burly
gunner clad in a brown sweater and a French
steel helmet, and carrying a long French

rifle, strolled across the road. The startling resemblance he bore to a Cromwellian soldier made us all turn out to see him.

Gunner Wolverhampton, as the archetype of his fellows, deserves more than passing notice. He had served twelve years in the regiment, had taken his discharge, and was in civilian employment when the war broke out. As soon as recruiting regulations allowed, that is about the third week of the war, he re-enlisted. These re-enlisted men were allotted regimental numbers from one upwards in the order in which they offered themselves, and Gunner Wolverhampton is justly proud of his single figure number. In appearance he is about forty-five, with a grave face, a well-built figure, and a slow and weighty method of speech. His peculiarity lies in his nose, which is a rich crimson —it must have been a most expensive acquisition. When asked his civilian trade, he gives it as sign-painter, a statement that once surprised one of his comrades into remarking *sotto voce*, " Gawd love us, chum, I thought you was a whisky-taster ! " An old soldier of the finest type, knowing all the ropes and imbued with that highest form of self-respect that only the traditions of the service can propagate, he is perfectly

invaluable by the mere force of his example
in these days when soldiers are turned out
by the million in a few months. A certain
proportion of the battery *matériel* and stores
were entirely in his hands, and he has never
throughout the campaign been found defi-
cient by so much as a pick-handle, nor has
his gun ever failed to be spotlessly clean and
in perfect order. Without the inclination
or necessary educational qualifications for
promotion, he is useful and contented as a
gunner, and in times of emergency the
whole of his section, including the non-com-
missioned officers themselves, instinctively
turn to him for guidance. He it is that
when the detachments are worn out after
a long period of digging or of working the
gun, keeps them hard at it by his example
and by caustic criticism of their relative
feebleness; he it was that walked calmly
down to where a neighbouring battery was
being shelled and led a party out, as though
he were taking some friends to get a drink, to
where the shells were falling viciously round
two or three wounded men, bringing them
in with utter unconcern for his own danger.
Ah, Gunner Wolverhampton, if this war
makes of all who serve in it men such as you,
then the cost of it in blood and treasure will

be as nothing when set by the side of the freshly won strength of a nation rejuvenated !

Happy hours are those spent just behind the line between the strenuous days of strife, when one feels merely a spectator of the pageantry of war, when one can study men at their best, for the strain of war brings out the good qualities of human nature and atrophies the bad. Hours they are of leisure, when one may drive into a town of perhaps some considerable local importance, where, even under the strange forms that war has cast upon it, the old peace-time life of the community yet lives. Not all the jostling crowd of khaki, the long trains of supply columns that block the narrow mediæval streets of Béthune, have essentially altered the character of the place as the market-town of the neighbouring district; the old square tower, the graceful belfry, still look down upon a crowd of *gamins*, of hatless women and girls, of old men standing in the market-place. Only the young men are wanting, and their place is taken by this surging crowd of the young men of another nation. Commercially, all such towns must be reaping a golden harvest. See how every pastry-cook's window bears the legend " Tea Rooms," extending below it a tempting array of *pâtisserie* that would shame the best of those dreadful " tea-shops " of our native land. And, when sufficiently allured, elbow your way in amongst the hungry rabble that speak a curious tongue they believe to be French—it does not matter, the proprietress and her daughter learnt English long ago, and have now almost acquired this same curious tongue—and try to get a seat. So it is with all the shops, and the Frenchman, with his instinct to provide what is required, has contrived that the most exacting of these English officers with their innumerable and most peculiar wants, shall rarely go away unsatisfied. In such towns as these will be found the representatives of those peculiar units that are raised (or do they raise themselves?) apparently for the sole purpose of encumbering the roads. But perhaps in the villages is seen the more amusing side of international commerce. In the towns everybody seems to know by instinct what the soldier wants —I have heard a gunner ask for fried fish and chips in the vernacular of Newcastle, and get it—but in the villages considerable parleying is sometimes necessary. There is a story of a man who rode to a farmhouse where eggs were to be obtained, and de-

manded " oofs." But madame was unre-
sponsive. " Non compris, monsieur, peut-
être il veut du lait, de la beurre——? " Desperate, the man dismounted, and, picking
up his horse's foot, tapped it significantly.
" No, ma'am, not lay or burr, oofs, oofs,
can't you see? "

XII

A WAR MESS

MORE amusement is usually to be derived from the Battery Mess than from any other side of the not uninteresting life of the campaign. Let half-a-dozen officers of varying ages, temperaments and ideas be collected at random from half the civilized globe, and set them down in a situation where their only relaxation must be found in one another's company, and watch the result. It can readily be imagined that there are endless piquant possibilities, a vast field of quiet entertainment for the student of the lighter side of existence.

As a rule, for the care of its material side, some heavenborn genius arises from amongst the ruck of his fellows, whose well-ordered brain revels in the details of cooks, and ration beef and the most convenient hour for dinner. Happy is the mess in its possession of him, how willingly its members forego any say in the matters pertaining to sustenance, in how docile a spirit do they submit to his autocratic ruling that marmalade is to be kept for breakfast alone, that lunch shall consist of bully-beef and cheese ! Our own battery was blessed beyond its fellows in a tyrant of dazzling capabilities, who coaxed mysterious dishes, of course with the collusion of the mess-cook, from the most unpromising materials, who fed us bountifully from secret stores of his own such time as we wandered forlorn over the face of the land, who allowed no comment upon the quality of the bacon or the resilience of the bread. We all looked blindly to him for our daily needs, much as the Children of Israel looked to Moses in the wilderness, and we were never disappointed. May his memory be for ever associated with these precious words—he fed us well !

Mess premises may be divided into two classes, the first being found in cases where the battery position is in a locality where the inhabitants are still in occupation of their houses, and consisting of some room in an *estaminet* or farm-house, the second being improvised in a ruin or dug-out. Both are capable of providing both trouble and comfort, in both a stern resolution to

o

take things cheerfully as they come results
wonderfully quickly in the discovery that
one is getting on very well considering.   I
have a vivid picture in my memory of a
mess of the first type, once the public room
of an *estaminet*, now given over for our use.
A few chairs and a table furnished it, its
doors opened upon a courtyard of extraordinary capabilities in the way of mud,
wherein stood the battery car, a horse or
two, and several fowls, one or more of which
items one invariably fell over in the dark.
Next to the mess-room was the kitchen,
of whose stove we had the use, and wherein
perpetually *madame* and the two mess
servants bickered for space for their culinary
operations.   And yet perhaps we were even
more comfortable in a home that we made
for ourselves in an abandoned miner's
cottage.   We glazed the windows, repaired
the shell-holes in the roof, stole doors and
a stove, and made the place thoroughly
weatherproof and comfortable.   And then,
the furnishing and decoration !   No newly-
engaged couple, who, if we may believe the
posters, spend their hours of bliss in arguing
whether they shall confide their savings to
Messrs. Deal & Glue or to the Houndsditch
Furnishing Co., ever furnished with such

a zest as did we. Abandoned villages lay
all around us, ours was the freedom to loot
as we would. The only trouble was that
we were by no means the first comers—
" our wants had all been felt, our errors
made before "—and it required diligent
search to find anything of any use. Our
wheeler mended a broken table, two triumphant servants struggled in with a gigantic
sideboard, the roofless and abandoned church
was raided for cane-seated chairs, we de-
scended like vultures upon a rival mess
when the battery that owned it, being
ordered to another position, abandoned it.
Growing ambitious, we refused to be contented with mere use, our cultivated taste
demanded ornament, decoration of the bare
walls, and our craving was gratified. Out
of every house we took the marvellous
examples of the photographer's art that
we found there, wonderful enlargements of
the owner, his wife, his children, in their
Sunday best, and hung them indiscriminately,
the more prepossessing " on the line," the
rest grouped with artistic abandon. Should
their exiled owners ever return to them,
what delight will be theirs to find those
two old enemies Monsieur Malbranque and
Madame Rietz hanging lovingly side by

side, or that stern old maid, Mademoiselle
Dalbine, surrounded by a group of mis-
cellaneous children ! What litigation may
not ensue when Madame Apelghem finds
her mahogany chest-of-drawers in Madame
Puchon's cellar, or Monsieur Verlane his
brand-new cooking-stove firmly cemented
into the bedroom of that doubtful lady
Ma'm'selle Frisson ! With what regret did
we leave this homelike mess to take the road
once more, and with what true instinct did
the senior subaltern insist upon the loading
into the last lorry of the best loved of the
portraits, so that it might follow the battery
in all its wanderings as a perpetual memory
of happy days ! It was a truly fearsome
enlargement of a terribly ugly little girl,
her face, with the mouth hanging open,
bearing an expression of acute agony, her
hands crossed over the region where the
pain might be expected to be, her toes
turned in despondently. " The Flatulent
Child " we christened her, yet perhaps none
of us, gazing into those inexpressive eyes,
can fail to remember days whose happiness
will always be a precious memory to us all.

The food question practically solves itself;
rations of surpassing quality are provided
in quantities that tax the keenest appetite

to consume, all that remains is to cook
them and to provide such delicate extras
as may be desired. And in that same
provision of extras there lies many a snare.
France is not a desert and savage land,
as, judging by the preparations that a con-
scientious mess secretary makes before he
embarks, one might expect to find it, and
nearly everything that one wants can be
obtained in the towns behind the line at
very reasonable prices. We had arranged
with a large firm in England to send us
fortnightly supplies, and there our troubles
began. The firm played their part nobly,
and beginning with the day we set out upon
our adventures, sent regularly the fortnightly
consignments. But heavy artillery owes
no allegiance to division or army corps,
but wanders like some distended bumble-
bee about the line, sipping honey in the shape
of rations now from this point, now from
that, until the Military Forwarding Officers,
the Railway Transport Officers, and all the
host of curiously termed people whose
business it is to play trains in this dis-
tracted land, lose all count of the whereabouts
of any particular battery. The result of
this to us was that for six weeks after our
arrival in France we heard nothing of our

long-expected delicacies, despite frantic
journeys to railhead after railhead, and
piteous applications to supply officers all
over the country. By this time we had
learnt that we could get what we wanted
close at hand, and had ceased to worry
about them, when one day we received a
message that some stores were awaiting us
at a certain station forty miles away.
Seizing a favourable opportunity, we dashed
over there in the battery car and secured
the first consignment, and being by that
time fairly well settled, we left instructions
for the forwarding of any subsequent lots
that might turn up. Then the accumulation of the fruitless weeks began to pour
in upon us. At every tactical crisis the
ration-lorry would dash up to the battery,
amidst a tempest of shot and shell, and
unload numberless cases of things of which
we already had a superfluity. Box after
box was dumped upon us, packed tight
with tins of cold and sodden fruit, of strange
cereal foods, of desiccated and strange-
tasting soups. Who, in a country where
food is treated as a fine art, would wish
to live upon such things ? Yet our stern
tyrant, his mind rebelling at the mere
thought of waste, ordained that it must

be so, and so it was. Alas, for the flesh-pots
of France, the omelettes and coffee of
Madame ! How tragic that you must vanish
to appear no more !

Of sleeping quarters much might be
written. What in theory could be more
delightful than to sleep in one's valise in
the open air—the thing is supposed to be
waterproof—to wake up fresh in the early
morning and roll on the dewy grass by way
of a bath ? What indeed ? The romance
of the proceeding appeals to the man allured
by the specious prospect of campaigning,
and he invariably attempts it for a few
nights, until he grows strangely silent towards
bed-time and furtively steals away to some
billet he has found. After that he fluctuates
between spreading his valise in a chicken-
run (it was night when we spread out our
valises, and the major's language on discovering in the morning that he had been
trying to hatch out a likely-looking brood
of chickens was, to put it respectfully,
bracing) and crawling luxuriously, in the
full glory of pyjamas, between real sheets.
The valise itself is all right, there is nothing
more comfortable, the only trouble is that
it is bed and portmanteau combined, so
that one's night's rest is shared by all one's

belongings, including one's spare pair of
boots. And I never met a pair of boots
in such circumstances that had not the
power of being in several places at once,
till one's valise, whichever way one turned,
did not seem to be as closely packed with
boots as a cobbler's shop. I repeat, the
valise is all right, that is if one's servant
knows how to fold the blankets in it, and
how to dispose the softer of its contents
under one's head. But the occasional
luxury of a real bed is very welcome, only
—treat the casual mattress with caution
until you know it thoroughly. If etymology
means in Flanders the study of the language
of the trenches, entomology is likewise the
study of a doubtful mattress, and both
sciences are often more extensive than it
would appear. Better in most billets is
the bare floor with a valise upon it than
the most tempting bed. Usually, however,
one has to use both. For many nights two
of us occupied a room exactly six feet by
eight, more than half of which was occupied
by the bed. Our process of turning-in was
interesting and extremely scientific. We
had tossed up for the bed, and my friend
had won it, so he retired to rest first. When
he was safely in bed, I came in, put all the

remaining furniture outside the door, shut
it, laid down my valise, and crawled into
it, my head jammed against the door, and
my feet up the stove pipe, like Alice in the
house of the White Rabbit.   He slept with his
feet out of the window, until early one morning a passing horse, of inquisitive tempera-
ment, seeing the blanket, gave it a sharp
tug. My friend woke up convinced the
Huns were upon us.

My most comfortable nights were spent
in a coal cellar, which two of us had cleared
out and adapted to our uses. My stable
companion, being something of a sybarite,
looted an iron bedstead on which to spread
his valise—it was a new and improved type,
and when extended in all its glory had a
curious canopy of its own, the effect of the
whole being like nothing so much as Noah's
Ark. Into this, with much difficulty and
objurgation he would crawl, when the
mysterious concern would promptly convert
itself into a portable washingstand or some
other fitment of extreme utility, whence it
had to be coaxed into the Ark-like form
again. I, less ambitious, supported a
shutter on some bricks, and laid my very
ordinary valise on that. It was far less
ostentatious, and I had fewer adventurous

nights. It was cold in that cellar, so we raided a stove that we lit every evening, finding plenty of broken rafters in the ruined houses round us to serve for fuel. We shall neither of us know again such nights as those, lulled to sleep as we were by the sleepless batteries around us, although in profound peace we might rest in the most sumptuous bed that Tottenham Court Road ever produced.

In this ideal spot we had a bathroom with a huge stove in it, on which to boil many gallons of water in petrol cans, and no luxury could equal the luxury of those hot baths. There was a tragedy connected with it, though. One young officer was wallowing in a glorious sea of foaming lather, when a shell burst a few yards from the door. Not being sure where and when to expect the next, he dashed as he was through the battery to his dug-out, the soap-suds flying from him as foam from the limbs of some swift-footed sea-god. Nor was the major more fortunate. Condemned to spend many weary days and nights in his O.P., and missing the bathroom, he constructed one on the same plan, but less the stove, in the house he used for the purpose. But unfortunately there was only

a wooden partition between him and the
enemy, and one day stray bullets began to
come through this with alarming frequency.
He, too, was compelled to beat a hurried
retreat.

Strange, too, are the messes that two or
three officers, alone together on detachment,
establish for their own convenience. I
know of one in the dark low hall of an old
farmhouse, that is in itself mess-room,
kitchen and sleeping apartment for the
servants of the two officers who lived in
the little room opening off it. Life there
was very much as we imagine it in mediæval
times, the officers had their meals with their
servants standing behind their chairs—not
from a desire for wanton display, but
because there was nowhere else to go—by
the light of two candles and the red glow
of the stove in the background. Upon
the oaken beams of the ceiling hung strange
shapes that were the implements of war,
looted German rifles and bayonets, haver-
sacks, water-bottles, binoculars, sextants and
other lethal weapons. A dripping oilskin
dried by the fire, the faint smell of warm
wet gum-boots mingled with that of the
boiling cabbage. Perhaps the telephone
that buzzed incessantly introduced a modern

element, but everything else, seen in the gloom of the shaded candles, looked ghostly, unreal, a scene from some forgotten haunt of a robber baron. And the rats ran fearlessly across the floor, or sat very still in the corners, their fierce eyes shining as the light caught them. Tea was the meal of the day in that mess, for then one of the two came in from his observation post at Suicide Corner, for which he had set out at half-past five in the morning, tired and hungry, and tea when the light has failed and the rising mist of late autumn foretells a white frost is a worthy meal. Suicide Corner was a bleak spot, too, and eight hours in such a place with nothing but bully-beef sandwiches for lunch gives one an amazing appetite. And if one's companion is Scotch with an apparently limitless acquaintance who send him shortbread and oat-cake, then one's cup of delight is full indeed.

Suicide Corner is not the name of that cross-roads where the observation post stands, but, as it stands there still, or part of it does at all events, its real name is best left unsaid. A feeble imitator of the immortal "Ruthless Rhymes" in his intervals of observation produced the following—

To a cross-roads that I know
Careful Colonels rarely go.
'Tis a pity; if the sniper
Potted men whose years were riper,
Our artillery promotion
Would be quicker, I've a notion!

and was wounded in that very spot on the next morning, which possibly he richly deserved. Yet close by was the Hidden Garden, a little plot of a few square feet hidden from prying eyes by a thick hedge, wherein grew chrysanthemums that were a never-failing delight to a pair of eyes tired of the ugliness of war's destruction, and a bush of rosemary that smelt of our own West Country. What loving hand had planted it, and will the owner of that hand return some day to find all the familiar houses in heaps of blackened ruins, the well-known trees cut down or mutilated by shell-fire, the peaceful fields furrowed with long trenches and strewn with fragments of shell? If so, perhaps the little garden will still show signs of the unknown who, in return for the beauty with which it gladdened his heart, tore up the weeds that bid fair to choke it and tended the flowers as best he could. And perhaps the very hand that planted the flowers will, on a more peaceful November 1, lay a bunch of them on each of the nameless graves that lie near by. And perhaps Suicide Corner will again become the centre of a wayside village, and the troubled air will forget the ceaseless song of the sniper's bullet and the sharp crack of rifle and roar of bursting shell. Only the thickly strewn graves will remain, witnesses that over this quiet spot was once the hunting-ground of Death.

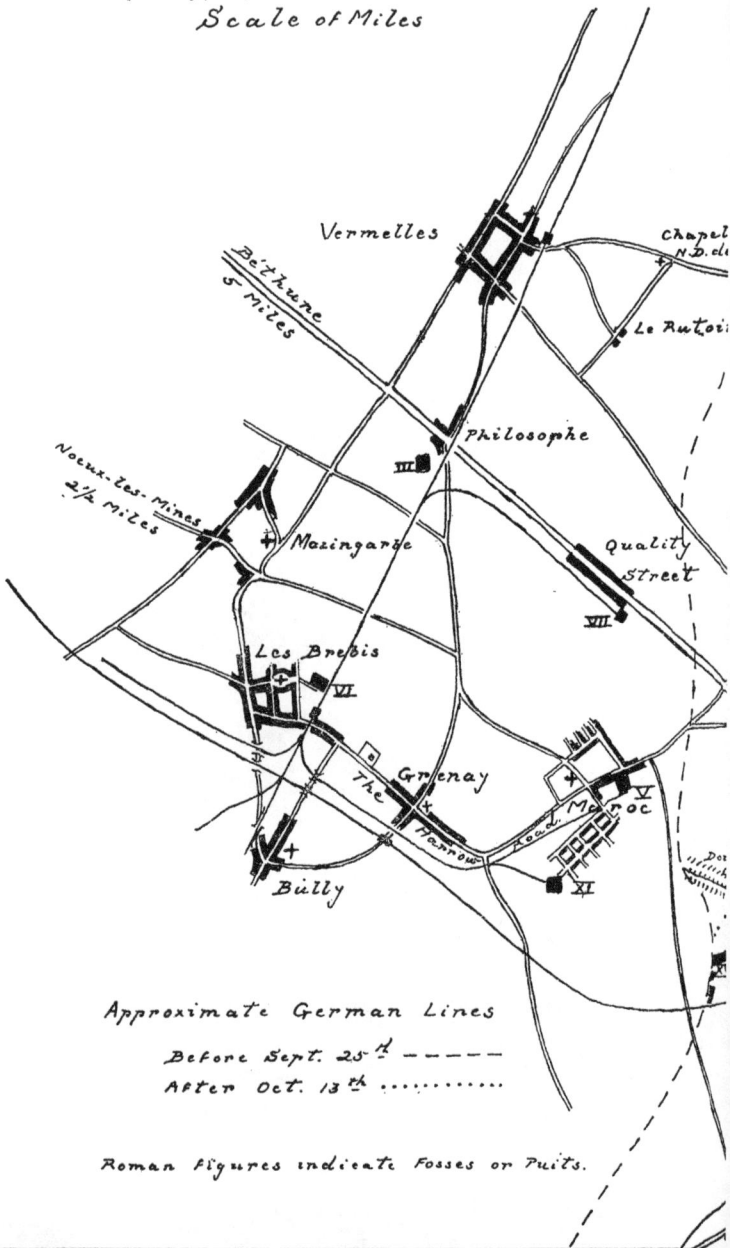

Scale of Miles

¾ ½ ¼ 0   1

Vermelles

Chapel
N.D. de

Béthune
5 Miles

Le Rutoi

Philosophe

Noeux-les-Mines
2½ Miles

Mazingarbe

Quality
Street

VII

Les Brebis

VI

Grenay

V
Maroc

The
Harrow

Road

XI

Bully

Approximate German Lines

Before Sept. 25ᵗʰ ‒ ‒ ‒ ‒ ‒

After Oct. 13ᵗʰ ....

Roman Figures indicate Fosses or Puits.

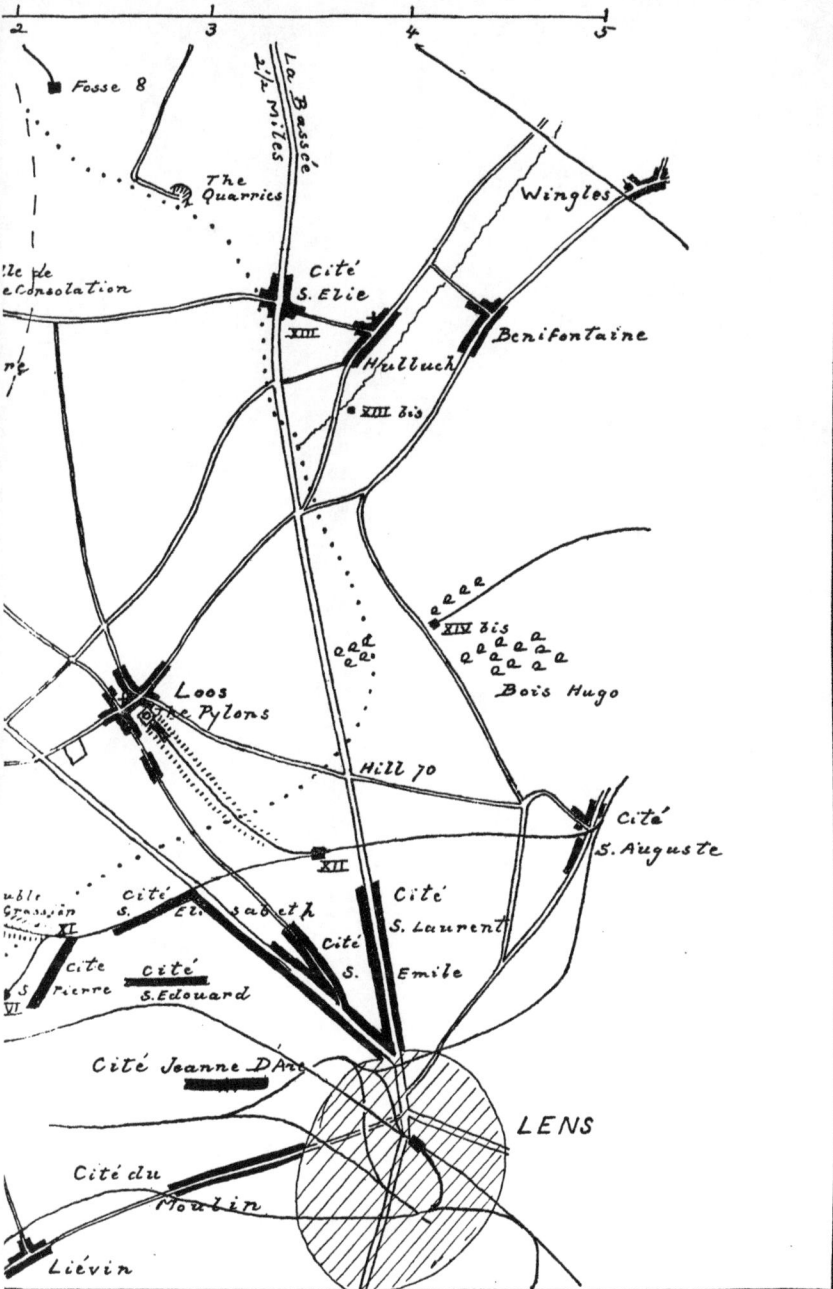

Country round Loos

2   3   4   5

Fosse 8

La Bassée 2½ miles

The Quarries

Wingles

..le de .e Consolation

Cité S. Elie

n..

XIII

Benifontaine

Hulluch

XIII bis

XIV bis

Bois Hugo

Loos Cité Pylons

Hill 70

Cité S. Auguste

XII

uble Grassier XI

Cité S. Elisabeth

Cité S. Laurent

Cité S. Emile

Cité Pierre

S. VI

Cité S. Edouard

Cité Jeanne D'Arc

LENS

Cité du Moulin

Liévin